THE
AWAKENING
CALL

FOSTERING INTIMACY WITH GOD

THE AWAKENING CALL

JAMES FINLEY

author of *Merton's Palace of Nowhere*

AVE MARIA PRESS   Notre Dame, Indiana

First printing, November 1984
Second printing, April, 1986
42,000 copies in print

Scripture texts used in this work are taken from
The New American Bible, The Jerusalem Bible and
The Revised Standard Version.

Excerpt from *The Cloud of Unknowing* by William Johnston.
Copyright © 1973 by William Johnston. Reprinted by permission of
Doubleday & Company, Inc.

From *The Collected Works of St. John of the Cross* translated by
Kieran Kavanaugh and Otilio Rodriguez, ICS Publications, 2131
Lincoln Road, N.E., Wash., D.C. 20002, 1979.

Library of Congress Catalog Card Number: 84-72094

International Standard Book Number: 0-87793-278-6

Printed and bound in the United States of America

Cover photograph by: H. Armstrong Roberts

Cover and text design by: Elizabeth J. French

To Kaye

ACKNOWLEDGMENTS

I wish to thank the following people, each of whom made unique contributions to these reflections. For their fidelity to prayer, their friendship and their insightful suggestions I am deeply grateful:

Sister Francis Therese Woznicki, S.S.J., Brother Anthony Distefano, O.C.S.O., John Finney, Carolyn Kerr, Sister Jane Marie Richardson, S.L., E. Springs Steele, Thomas Barnes, Brother John Rounds, O.C.D., Sister Therese Sedlock, O.S.F., and Sister Lucille Myers, S.I.W.

I am indebted to Reverend Timothy Kelly, abbot of Gethsemani, for permission to quote from the Dan Walsh material, to the staff of Ave Maria Press for their support and encouragement, and to all who have listened to my conferences in which I first formulated the themes explored in these pages.

Becky Knapp did an excellent job of typing the final draft of the manuscript.

JAMES FINLEY

CONTENTS

PREFACE

These reflections intuitively explore the transformations that mysteriously unfold in the hearts of those seeking deeper intimacy with God in prayer. More specifically, they consist of my personal exploration into these transformations. The book is, in effect, my prayer journal, which I wrote to enhance my efforts to clarify for myself my own journey toward God in prayer. Thus, what I offer in these pages are not the answers of an expert in prayer, but rather glimpses into the searchings of a fellow pilgrim.

I experienced the writing of these reflections to be somewhat like tuning a musical instrument. A tuning fork is struck and then a string of the instrument is plucked and slowly tightened as one searches for the sound that begins to resonate with that of the fork. Similarly, in the ongoing process of writing reflections such as these I rise early for prayer. And in the silence there is an image—not necessarily a visual image, sometimes it is more an inner certitude, a kind of inner truth. Then I slowly, prayerfully search for a word or a pattern of words that keeps getting "tuned" until it begins to resonate with what is interiorly, obscurely known.

This book has structure. It contains chapters and paragraphs, each devoted to a specific theme or idea, which I feel to be of significance in the development of a contemplative way of life. But my own perception of these reflections is not that of a series of conceptual propositions, but instead is that of a tenuous instrument intended to resonate with things unseen. Or perhaps I should say my perception of these reflections is that of a long poem in blank verse about God, who, in his love for us, draws us in every moment into an incomprehensible union with himself.

As noted, these reflections are not simply a series of vertical, poetic searchings intended to sound, however feebly, the depths of the mystery of intimacy with God in prayer. They are as well a biographical endeavor, an attempt to explore the formative influences of my own spiritual journey. In this horizontal, biographical sense, these reflections are a continuation of a process begun in my book *Merton's Palace of Nowhere* (Ave Maria Press, 1978), where I explored what I gained in my exposure to Thomas Merton as my spiritual teacher and guide. Here in this book I turn from Merton to other formative influences of my own intuitive convictions about what it means to be faithful to God in prayer.

Two of these formative influences are the writings of St. John of the Cross and the anonymously written 14th-century Christian classic, *The Cloud of Unknowing*. Nearly every chapter of this book contains a section devoted to reflecting upon passages taken from *The Cloud of Unknowing* and/or the writings of St. John of the Cross. No attempt is made in these sections to explain the synthesis unique to each of these two spiritual masters. Instead, I examine their writings in an attempt to get in touch with their formative influence on my own life. During a two-year period, while I was a monk at Gethsemani, I read practically nothing other than scripture, philosophy, *The Cloud of Unknowing* and St. John of the Cross. In a very personal sense, the author of *The Cloud of Unknowing* and St. John of the Cross fed me and left their mark upon me. I refer to them here not to explain them in conceptual terms, but rather to renew for myself and to share with you, the reader, what I gained in my exposure to their wisdom concerning the one thing necessary.

A third formative influence explored here is the teaching of Daniel Walsh, Thomas Merton's lifelong friend and mentor and my philosophy professor at Gethsemani. Drawing primarily from St. Augustine, the Franciscan school as represented by Duns Scotus, and the Cistercian school as represented by St. Bernard and William of St. Thierry, Dan Walsh developed what he called a philosophy of the person. This philosophical meditation on the mystery of our creation in God's image and likeness contributed significantly, I think, to Merton's notion of the true self. It contributed as well to my own spiritual development. I restricted explicit reference to Walsh's teaching to one section of Chapter five. But his influence is present in this book in every reference to the primacy of love in God's personal creation and to the Self fashioned in that love.

The inner journey that is the subject matter of these reflections is a simple thing, really, too simple to talk about without in some way turning it into something other than it is. It has to do with being in love with God. It has to do with the possibility of a transforming breakthrough into an obscure realization of one's perfect union with God in Christ. It has to do with being poor enough to live such that one's whole life somehow depends on being faithful to God in prayer.

I must tell you that I am not faithful. Even as I write this Preface I am aware that at times the writing of these pages about prayer was my way of evading prayer. At times, too, I continue to get lost in a schedule in which there are always more things to do than there is time to do them in. But this book has been a gift to me. It has served as a centering place, a point of return back to God's call for us to live in the awareness of his life-sustaining presence. Truly, this is why I share these pages with you. I share them in the hope that they will serve as a centering place for you as well, a point of contact with the great and simple truth of God's will for us to be one with him.

INTRODUCTION

While giving meditation retreats I have the opportunity to speak privately with many people about their spiritual lives. Over and over again I have heard in these conversations a single refrain repeated in countless variations. This refrain is that of a felt desire for deeper intimacy with God in prayer. Sometimes the desire is gentle and pervasive, moving a person toward spending some time alone each day simply *to be* or to paint, or garden, or engage in some other simple activity that allows them to collect themselves in God's presence. Sometimes the desire is more centered and intense, coming in the form of an ache that stirs in the heart, moving the person toward a radical union with God in silence.

The people with whom I speak are "just like everybody else." There is nothing extraordinary about them in the sense that they live ordinary lives in the world of spilled coffee and burnt toast doing their best to live as happy, productive, sane people in loving, caring relationships with those around them. They see themselves as beginners in the spiritual life. When it comes to prayer they have more questions than they have answers. But in the midst of all these contingencies there burns within a delicate, subtle fire—a desire without name that they intuit to be the presence of God calling them to union with himself. They know that for them being a disciple of the risen Lord means learning to live in fidelity to this desire by seeking its fulfillment in everything they do. And it is in this discipleship of the inner way that they seek guidance in prayer.

These reflections are written in the hope of providing a source of encouragement and guidance to all who have tasted this desire and seek its fulfillment in their lives. The guidance offered is not particularly that of describing practical methods of prayer, for it is assumed here that at its hidden center prayer is never primarily something we do in a certain way. Rather, it is a way of being in God's presence which entails all the saving impracticality of the cross. Moreover, the guidance offered here is not in the form of theological concepts that define the nature of prayer. For it is assumed that prayer necessitates the leaving behind of all concepts, considered as absolutes capable of defining our relationship with God and how it is to be achieved.

The guidance offered is intended neither to describe or prescribe. Rather, the intent is to evoke the simple faith awareness in which the divine plea, "Be still and know that I am God" (Ps 46:10), can be heard and followed with childlike confidence. The guidance is that of coaxing the reader toward that act of self-surrender to God in which God awakens us to who we are in his love.

This book is not so much something to study as it is something you might decide to tuck under your arm to take with you on a walk. Then, sitting momentarily on a rock to rest and pray, you might decide to read a few pages, knowing full well the book has no more to tell you than the rock does. It has nothing to offer except to urge you to follow the promptings of your heart by turning inwardly to God, trusting that he will bring to fulfillment the desire for him that he has placed within you.

If you ask me just precisely how one is to go about doing the contemplative work of love, I am at a complete loss. All I can say is I pray that Almighty God in his great goodness and kindness will teach you himself. For in all honesty I must admit I do not know. And no wonder, for it is a divine activity and God will do it in whomever he chooses. No one can earn it. Paradoxical as it may seem, it would not even occur to a person—no, nor to an angel or saint—to desire contemplative love were it not already alive within him. I believe, too, that often our Lord deliberately chooses to work in those who have been habitual sinners rather than in those who, by comparison, have never grieved him at all. Yes, he seems to do this very often. For I think he wants us to realize that he is all-merciful and almighty, and that he is perfectly free to work as he pleases, where he pleases, and when he pleases.

The Cloud of Unknowing

1 WHAT IS CONTEMPLATIVE PRAYER?

Both scripture and tradition reveal to us that our very existence has its origin, foundation and fulfillment in a divine call to share in God's life. Our faith is our personal awakening and response to this call. The deeper our faith the more keenly is felt the need to give ourselves entirely to God, who gives himself entirely to us in creating us moment by moment in his image and likeness for himself alone. Our faith awakens in us the awareness of God's self-giving love and thus sets in motion a reciprocity of love in moving us to give ourselves to God with all the loving abandon in which he gives himself to us.

Prayer is the incarnation of faith. Whatever particular form prayer takes, its essence is that of a heartfelt, interior bonding of one's self to God in the faith awareness of God's gratuitous love in which he eternally binds himself to us.

What then is contemplative prayer? One way to respond to this question is by defining the mode of consciousness termed contemplation which characterizes it. Such an approach, while logical, is nevertheless problematic in that contemplation by its very nature tends to evade clear conceptualization. The dictionary definition of contemplation ("to look at or view with continued attention; observe thoughtfully") is conceptually accurate but leaves what is essential unsaid. Like an X-ray of one's mother that shows what is true, while leaving out the loving expression on her face, a conceptual definition fails to communicate that qualitative existential richness given in a quiet moment under the stars or before a great work of art. It seems that no matter how astute one's definition of the depths of awareness given in such moments might be, there always remains an undefinable element that we intuit to be the very core of the experience.

The question, What is contemplation? resembles such questions as, What is being? What is the mind? or What is love? The resemblance lies in the fact that these and similar questions do not refer to realities that can be readily looked upon as objects external to ourselves, such as an automobile tire or a newspaper. Instead, such questions refer to the unseen, spiritual dimensions of the "I" that is asking the question. Contemplation, in other words, is an expression of the spiritual dimension of our being and as such cannot be completely objectified in a definition without at the same time being in some way falsified.

Turning specifically to the contemplation of God only serves to heighten the inadequacy of conceptual definitions. God is neither a thing of nature nor another finite human being. He is the ALL, the one from whom all things come and in whose image and likeness all persons are created. The obscure taste of intimacy with God given in contemplative prayer cannot be known by the conceptualizing mind except through analogies and negations, all of which fail to provide more than frail "hints and guesses" of the divine gift they attempt to convey.

If a direct conceptual approach of trying to define contemplative prayer is troublesome, we can turn to a less direct but also less problematic approach to understanding something of what contemplative prayer is by comparing it to other forms of prayer. Traditionally, contemplative prayer has been seen as the culmination of a graced evolution of consciousness in which one moves from *spiritual reading* to *meditation* to *contemplation*.

Spiritual reading as a form of prayer might be experienced in this way: You go to a quiet place, and taking a few moments to relax and to let go of whatever it is that might be preoccupying you at the moment, you interiorly turn to God. You express your faith that you are in his presence and that he is about to speak to you in his word. Then, opening the scriptures you begin to read, "My shepherd is the Lord. There is nothing I shall want. . . ." More precisely, you pray the words in allowing the Lord who is your shepherd to speak to your heart of his providential love in which he eternally watches over you in this moment of prayer. Thus, by reading the scriptures in a spirit of faith you enter into a kind of meeting place with God in which you become more aware of and responsive to his loving presence in your daily life.

Spiritual reading has within it an inner momentum that carries you from spiritual reading into *meditation*. You read, "My shepherd is the Lord. There is nothing I shall want. . . ." And instead of moving on to the next verse, you pause and in your own words begin spontaneously to pray to the Lord, saying, "Why, Lord, do I want so much? Teach me to follow you. Teach me to understand that you are, in truth, my shepherd, and that in your love for me I lack nothing. . . ." In meditation the words of scripture serve as a point of departure for a personal exploration into how God's living word—his risen

Son—is uniquely present and active in your daily life and relevant to its deepest, hidden purposes.

Meditation gives way to *contemplation* in moments in which your reading and meditation awakens a simple desire to commune with God as he mysteriously makes his presence felt within you. In contemplative prayer you do not simply open the scriptures and pray the words, "Be still and know that I am God." Nor do you meditate on what this stillness might be. Instead, you *are* still. Touched by God's presence you rest (perhaps fleetingly and obscurely) in the faith awareness of that union with God that is eternal life.

In meditation the discursive intellect and imagination are active in a personal awareness of specific aspects of the mystery of our union with God in Christ. In contemplation, however, both the discursive intellect and the imagination are silenced and transcended in an utterly simple moment of loving communion with God as he is in himself. Contemplation is marked by naked faith, presence and radical intimacy. It is marked, too, by ineffability—by an all-embracing totality that defies the limitations of a description. If images are focused upon in contemplative prayer, they tend to appear as transparent, archetypal images that give birth to spiritual consciousness. If words are used, they tend to take on the quality of words or phrases repeated over and over within the heart as evocations of the Spirit-given awareness of the living God. That is, both words and images are used as focal points of transformation in which one is awakened to spiritual processes unfolding from within.

An analogy to the progression from spiritual reading to contemplation can be found in the example of a man reading a love letter. He begins to read attentively as a way of drawing closer to the one whose words touch his heart (spiritual reading). As he reads, he pauses, for her words initiate a reverie of love in which is set free a hundred hopes and images (meditation). As he reads, the one who wrote the letter unexpectedly walks into the room. He looks up at her, saying nothing (contemplation).*

There is yet another approach to our present attempts at responding to the question, What is contemplation?; namely, that of presenting a parable:

Imagine a woman walking alone in the woods, searching for her lost child. Suddenly, in the distance, she hears what sounds like a faint cry for help. Just as suddenly she stops, for now the noise of the dry leaves beneath her feet is an intolerable interference. So strong is her love that for a brief moment she stops breathing. She is a listening presence. And in the silence a faint cry is heard that makes her heart leap.

You sit alone slowly reading the scriptures. In a way you do not understand, and in a manner so subtle you cannot grasp it, there begins to grow in you a gentle, persistent desire for intimacy with God. It is as though you are reading the scriptures not so much to understand the words as to keep alive and nurture this listening. Or, perhaps, it is that each word, when spiritually understood, is perceived as a call to listen—to be faithfully attentive to a great desire that consumes you in the emptiness and yet holds you there in the emptiness, vanishing the moment you turn to look at it.

---

*When concerned specifically about the progression from meditation to contemplation I will maintain this classical distinction between these two forms of prayer. Generally, however, the terms meditation, contemplation, as well as interior prayer, solitary prayer and other terms will be used interchangeably to denote a movement toward an ever greater degree of personal intimacy with God that forms the hidden foundation of all prayer.

The hidden center of the moment lies beyond what can be completely comprehended with the mind, or felt in the senses or the emotions. The hidden center of the moment is a union with God in which you are awakened and called to an ever-faithful sweetness, that your inmost Self intuitively recognizes and responds to in the felt need to remain still, open and attentive.

Here, every movement of the egocentric self becomes an intolerable interference. And yet to make deliberate efforts to be silent in forced or unnatural ways causes but more noise. The only thing you can do is let it happen. The only thing you can do is let God be God in yielding yourself over to his transforming presence by accepting your poverty, your helplessness to surrender. And here in this Spirit-born attentiveness there is heard—so faintly it is not there—the call that makes your heart leap in awakening in you that which is wholly virginal and wholly like God.

This call is said to be so faint it is not there because, being the call of God's ecstatic love, it is not heard in the domain of the multiplicity of things that appear before us. It is heard only in the domain of God, who is the ground, the abyss, the fontal unity that is never "out there" as a thing for us to see, hear or grasp at. The awakening call to contemplative intimacy with God is then the awakening of a graced awareness of a secret communion with God which obscurely and gratuitously begins to abide within us.

This obscure abiding of divine love draws us into a way of living that resembles the situation of the mother looking for her lost child. *Why* was she in the forest? What *kind* of forest was she in? She did not go into the forest in order to have experiences of herself looking for her lost child. She is in the forest because she is in love, because one whose presence within her heart is now somehow lost and hidden from her. This is the kind of forest she is in—the forest of leaving concern for one's self behind in following the call to union with one without whom life cannot go on. It is the place of love unfulfilled, a place where there is no rest save that of union with the one who draws us there, no beauty save the face of the one we seek. This is the domain of God. The place in which we sit in silent prayer.

2 AM I CALLED TO CONTEMPLATIVE PRAYER?

Phrasing the question asked in the title of this chapter in more general terms, we first ask ourselves the question, Is everyone called to contemplative intimacy with God? The answer is yes and no. In a sense, everyone is called to contemplative intimacy with God, and in another sense the call to contemplative prayer is a *charism,* given to some as a particular expression of our universal call to faith, hope and love.

Everyone is called to contemplation in the universal, ultimate sense that every person is first and last a contemplative. We are each first a contemplative in that our origin is God's eternal contemplation of us in the image of his ecstatic love. Forever beholding us there hidden in his love as imitable, he utters to us his *fiat* of creation. He brings into being through Christ the Word, the Self he calls us to be in his love. And each of us is lastly a contemplative in that we will finally become the person God calls us to be in his love only when we come to share perfectly in the Father and Son's contemplation of one another in the unity of the Holy Spirit.*

*As explained in the Preface, this and all similar statements about God's personal creation are made in reference to the teachings of Dan Walsh, which are presented in Chapter 5.

In continuity with this ultimate, personal call to contemplative union with God in his love, we are each a contemplative in the sense that our humanity (our means to personal fulfillment) is innately open to contemplation. Contemplation is natural to us. It is inherent in life itself: a small child lost in the joy of playing with water, lovers surrendered over to gazing into each other's eyes, that instinct in each of us that draws us, even for a fleeting moment, to listen without comment to the sound of a rushing stream—all reveal the contemplative dimensions of our humanity.

As applied to Christian life we can observe a universal contemplative dimension to our faith. Every Christian experiences at least a momentary taste of the need to be with God in a childlike, silent awareness of his loving presence. There is in the heart of every disciple the need to touch, however obscurely, a depth of simple communion with our Lord "closer to us than we are to ourselves" (Augustine).

In response, then, to the question, Am I called to contemplative prayer?, it can be answered, yes. I am a person, a human being, a Christian and thus I share God's call for all of his children to participate in Christ the Word's eternal contemplation of the Father in the unity of the Holy Spirit. I can then confidently seek to grow in this contemplative dimension of the heritage that is mine as a child of the Father.

The notion of contemplative prayer as a charism, a call given to some and not to others, is also present in the classical texts of the Christian contemplative traditions. Contemplative prayer as a charism can be said to refer to a phenomenon that appears in the life of some, but not all, Christians. This phenomenon is that of being in some way interiorly touched by the felt need to deepen one's wordless, intuitive awareness of intimacy with God in Christ. The call is perhaps best understood in terms of emphasis. That is, there are some people who experience a spontaneous gravitation toward an emphasis of seeking contemplative intimacy with God. The experience can be confusing, especially if it is newly encountered and one has no spiritual director with whom to explore and discern what is happening.

Traditionally, those who experienced this call were likely to follow in the footsteps of Sts. Benedict, Bernard, or Teresa of Avila by entering a cloistered, contemplative order. This, for some, remains a basic aspect of their response to the call to a life of deep interior prayer. Today, however, there seems to be a renewed awareness that this call is first and foremost not a call to live in a certain kind of social, religious institution. Rather, it is essentially a call to live one's daily life as claimed by God for a transforming intimacy with himself in a lifetime of fidelity to interior prayer.

This call comes to college students, housewives, insurance salesmen and prisoners. It comes to religious, diocesan priests, Protestant clergy and rabbis. It comes to whom it comes. It is given to whom it is given. We can ask for it with great desire (and to do so is a sign that most likely it has already been given). But we cannot make it happen. Like everything real, it simply comes to us. It simply appears as an unexpected gift. And in appearing, obscurely and secretly in the hidden recesses of our hearts, it awaits our response—our yes to the transforming union that is held out to us.

Here the question that arises is not the philosophical question, Is everyone called to contemplative prayer?, but rather the profoundly personal question, Am I called to contemplative prayer?

The last chapter of the 14th-century English classic, *The Cloud of Unknowing,* * is devoted exclusively to the question of discerning whether or not one is called to contemplative prayer. The anonymous author of this Christian masterpiece begins the final chapter of his book by stating:

> I would like to make clear that not everyone who reads this book or finds it pleasantly interesting is therefore called to contemplation. The inner excitement he may feel may not be so much the attraction of grace as the arousal of natural curiosity (chap. 75, p. 145).

The author of *The Cloud* then goes on to provide two signs by which one can discern whether or not an attraction to contemplative prayer is truly from God. First, he states:

> Let a man examine himself to see if he has done all in his power to purify his conscience of deliberate sin according to the precepts of Holy Church and the advice of his spiritual father (p. 145).

This "know thyself" word of advice suggests the need to step back from the immediate question concerning contemplative prayer to ask a much more basic and broader question concerning the whole of one's life in God's presence. The advice suggests that what is needed first in a genuine life of prayer is a genuine Christian life, a life completely given over to following God's will in all things. What can be deceptive regarding the desire for contemplation is what Kierkegaard calls an aesthetic ap-

---

*See William Johnston, trans. *The Cloud of Unknowing and the Book of Privy Counselling*. New York: Image Doubleday, 1973. Page references used here correspond to Johnston's translation.

proach to faith in which one is lured by the beauty or charm of certain beliefs or practices while at the same time clinging to sinful attitudes and actions quite opposed to a life of discipleship.

What matters here is that we have given our life completely to Christ and are doing everything in our power to live in conformity with our faith commitment. This, however, is not to be taken in a moralistic sense in thinking that one must first get a perfect moral report card before being called to contemplation. Quite the contrary, such a pharisaical notion fails to take into account the fact that we cannot cleanse ourselves of sin as a "fundamental choice against the good" that is lodged deep within us where only grace can reach (chap. 10, p. 62). This is why prayer as a heartfelt turning toward and surrender to God is the way to holiness: "The contemplative work of love by itself will eventually heal you of all the roots of sin" (chap. 12, p. 64).

Having established that the attraction to contemplative prayer is not simply a matter of curiosity or mere aesthetic attraction, the beginning contemplative should also be able to observe that the desire for contemplative prayer will,

> . . . leave him no peace in any exterior or interior
> work he does unless he makes this secret little love
> . . . his principal concern (p. 145).

A parish priest who neglects his parish, a religious who neglects his or her community, or a married man who neglects his wife and children can have no real peace in anything until they restore to their lives a fidelity to those with whom, by God's will, they are united. Similarly, suggests the author of *The Cloud,* the one called to contemplative prayer can abandon silent prayer only at the price of feeling an interior dissatisfaction with oneself, one's daily life and relationships with others. Somehow, everything is hollow and lacking in integrity until one returns to God in silence.

We have to do what we have to do. And to be called to contemplation means one has to be silent in the presence of God, not in the sense that God holds it as sinful if we do not, but in the sense that an unrequited love waits within. Thus, in a mysterious and subtle fashion, infidelity is at the origin of all we call evil—when God our Father approaches to be with us, we run from him and hide, and in this flight there is no peace.

How does this happen to a person that he or she finds that fidelity to some form of daily interior prayer has become an inner necessity? The divine imperative does not come to us from the outside as a directive or exhortation to pray, which we feel duty-bound to follow. Instead, the call to silent prayer originates deep within, where God dwells as the master of our lives. And yet in this subjective, highly personal sense, the call to intimacy with God surrounds us and beckons to us from beyond ourselves, from the point at which we dwell in God as wholly dependent on his creation of us in his love. It is hard to talk about—like a fog that imperceptibly fills a forest at night, the desire for intimacy with God permeates our lives. Then suddenly it can make itself felt with great, unexpected force:

Unable to sleep you get up in the middle of the night to read. As you read you feel the gentle impulse to pray. Putting down your book you begin with words that move you unexpectedly into a stark silence. The emptiness deepens, when suddenly a single petal falls from a vase of flowers, lighting upon the floor—and in a fleeting instant you taste something of God's ravaging, gentle nearness!

The moment is a birth. It is a death. It is nothing. It claims your heart, marks it with a question:

Is it possible that in fidelity to silent waiting everything I could ever hope to receive from God, and infinitely more, lies waiting for me? Is it possible that the nakedness and poverty of wordless prayer is my way, my discipleship to the risen Lord? Is it here in this silence that the Spirit waits with unutterable groanings to place on my lips the words, "I and the Father are one?" . . . Somehow, deep in your heart, you already know the answer. It is this conviction, rooted in experience, that will allow no true peace without fidelity to the inner way of contemplative prayer.

The author of *The Cloud* provides a third indication that one is being called by God to contemplative prayer:

> Let him see if he is habitually more attracted to this simple contemplative prayer than to any other spiritual devotion (p. 145).

The *habitual* attraction to contemplative prayer is not restricted to a desire for solitary silence, as might be experienced in the middle of the night. Instead, the habitual desire extends into a general tendency to gravitate toward the contemplative dimension of every prayer. Thus, for example, it is not that one stops reading the scriptures in order to enter into contemplative prayer. Instead, one experiences that the symphonic richness of scripture tends of its own accord to refine itself out into a single note of "silent music" that quickens and intensifies the desire for union with God. Similarly, attendance at the liturgy is not something one hurriedly gets through in order to have a few moments after communion for silent prayer. Instead, one stands in the believing community with eyes opened in the breaking of the bread to the presence of the beloved drawing us into communion with himself.

Nor is the habitual attraction to contemplative prayer isolated to times of prayer. Right in the midst of one's daily work there is given, at times, momentary flashes of the divine dimensions of the task at hand. The habitual tendency of which the author of *The Cloud* speaks is a tendency of the heart and mind to gravitate toward the center of the present moment, where God holds us in his embrace, sustaining us in existence for his love's sake. The habitual attraction amounts to a call to a way of life in which intuitive awareness of and sensitivity to the divine presence becomes one's fundamental modality of being in the world.

Taken in a literal, narrow sense, the above signs would seem to exclude many who, in their daily lack of any such desires, might be led to conclude that they have some major house cleaning to do before God would even consider coming to pay them a visit with an invitation to contemplative prayer. Many may feel their tendency to lose all track of God's presence in the push and pull of daily events excludes them from the ranks of those called to contemplation.

Perhaps such a conclusion is a valid one. Perhaps one's charisms lie elsewhere. The author of *The Cloud,* however, cautions against a too hasty conclusion that may not at all be true. Just as the attraction to contemplation does not necessarily mean one is called to it, neither does going for long periods devoid of any felt desire for contemplation mean one is not called to seek intimacy with God in prayer.

> I am not saying that those who are being called to contemplation will feel the stirring of love continually and permanently right from the beginning,

for such is not the case. In fact, the young contemplative apprentice may often completely cease
to experience it (p. 145).

The author of *The Cloud* does not stop simply with
the consoling bit of good news to reassure us that our on-
again, off-again awareness of God's presence is no
obstacle to intimacy with him in prayer. He goes on to
provide insight into *why* we tend to lose our awareness of
God's presence and the felt need to be one with him. One
reason, he writes, is that of our infidelity:

> God may withdraw this gift (the inner stirring of
> love) when the young apprentice grows careless and
> begins to take it for granted. If this happens he will
> very likely be overwhelmed with bitter pangs of
> remorse (p. 145).

Often we do not appreciate something until we face
the possibility of losing it. A bout with cancer, or a series
of events that bring a marriage or a religious vocation to
ruin can occasion a previously unknown sense of
gratitude for the giftedness of life.

This new appreciation can bring with it a genuine
sense of remorse over past carelessness. Here, the author
of *The Cloud* states that carelessness and presumption
with the gift of prayer can result in its being lost. God,
however, never fails us; our infidelity meets his unwaver-
ing fidelity in the gift of remorse in which he teaches us
the ways of his love.

Becoming yet more subtle in his reflection on why
one can lose the felt sense of God's presence and the
desire to be one with him, the author of *The Cloud* states:

> Sometimes God will withdraw it so he (the begin-
> ning contemplative) will not begin to presume it is

his own doing, or that he can control it as he likes. Presumption like this is pride. Whenever the feeling of grace is withdrawn, pride is the cause. Not necessarily because one has actually yielded to pride, but because if this grace were not withdrawn from time to time pride would surely take root. God in his mercy protects the contemplative in this way (p. 145).

Subject to the ignorance of original sin, we do not understand the nature of the union with God to which we are called, and consequently we tend not to understand what threatens our advance toward it. Subject to sin, our hearts are shot through with frailty. God in his wisdom knows us through and through. He knows of all we do not know concerning our own weaknesses and our need for his strength. He sees around every corner. For him the night is as clear as day. And in his providential wisdom and fatherly love *he protects us from pride even before pride actually appears.*

Here the author of *The Cloud* would remind us that contemplation is a gift, not an achievement. It is a transformation of our hearts resulting in an awakening to who we are in Christ that is carried out according to God's will and not our own. This is made evident in the way contemplation comes to us, like "the wind that blows where it pleases." By the same token, divine freedom that bestows the gift of contemplation is equally manifested in the way the felt desire for intimacy with God leaves us. Suddenly it is gone! And in its departure we can learn humility and detachment. We can learn to have gratitude to God for teaching us that the moments of our awareness of his presence truly are from him, as revealed in our helplessness to possess and control them. This, however, is not enough, for we must begin to learn

as well that the felt absence of God is itself the beginning
of a new, more spiritual relationship with him.

In order to appreciate the divine and providential
nature of these apparently unsolicited periods of feeling
devoid of any felt sense of a desire for intimacy with God,
attention must be directed away from the vacillations of
what we feel and do not feel, to the more abiding, interior
stance of our heart in God's presence. We have, in other
words, to consider the fruit that these periods of God's
apparent absence are bearing in our life. If the fruit is that
of making us more Christlike in our trusting of God's
ways, then we can have a sense of confidence that God is
leading us to union with himself.

Our ability to appreciate the unseen, divine harvest
that grows in periods of spiritual dryness is often
unrecognized until the moment when the gift of contemplative prayer returns. It is in our response to these
moments that we can discover both the true nature of our
time of spiritual dryness, as well as what the author of
The Cloud affirms to be the surest sign that one is called
to contemplation:

> For if after long delay and inability to do this work
> (simple, contemplative prayer) he feels his desire for
> it renewed with greater passion and a deeper long-
> ing of love—so much so that (as I often think) the
> sorrow he felt at its loss seems like nothing at all
> beside his joy at finding it again—he need have no
> fear of error in believing that God is calling him to
> contemplation, regardless of what sort of person he
> is now or has been in the past. It is not what you are
> nor what you have been that God sees with his all-
> merciful eyes, but what you desire to be (p. 146).

When a man and woman think they have fallen in
love in sharing a moment of intimacy and then become

parted for a long time, the truth of their love is revealed
in the moment they meet again. If the love they shared
was no more than a feeling, then meeting again occasions
no more than feelings associated with memories of what
once was but is no more. But if their love is genuine,
meeting again occasions an indescribable joy. So, too,
says the author of *The Cloud,* going for a long period of
time without being able to enter into contemplative communion with God but sets the stage for the true contemplative to discover anew the joy of being claimed by
divine love.

It is such a simple thing, and yet it is the gift impossible to comprehend:

You sit in prayer, perhaps reading the scriptures,
perhaps not. When, in a secret instant, you unexpectedly
yield your inmost Self to God as he receives you into
himself. In the moment of rediscovered union you silently
cry out from the depths of your heart: "Why have I been
so foolish not to realize that everything in me desires the
fulfillment of this union with you and nothing else, ab-
solutely nothing else. For this is what I desire to be. This
is who I truly am—one marked, claimed and surrendered
over to your love."

The joy of rediscovered love unveils the Self God
forever beholds in his love, for *it is the Self he creates for*
himself alone through Christ the Word by calling us to
share in all the Word is. The joy of rediscovered love also
unveils the true nature of God's apparent absence. He only *seemed* to go away so that we could experience our
poverty and nothingness without him. He withdraws our
awareness of his presence only to create an empty place in
us, consisting of our desire for his return. It is on this
point the author of *The Cloud* ends this final chapter of
his book in quoting St. Augustine as saying, "The entire

life of a good Christian is nothing less than holy desire.''
And he quotes St. Gregory in clarifying the nature of this
desire: "All holy desires heighten in intensity with the
delay of fulfillment, and desire which fades with delay
was never holy desire at all" (p. 146).

In our poverty our desire for God *seems* to fade as a
kind of reflection of God, who *seems* to leave us. But the
joy we experience with each renewed awareness of God's
presence reveals in us an invincible, hidden desire that we
are not allowed to see. If we could go about constantly
aware of our desire for God, we would always be prone to
self-infatuation. What we feel most of the time is our
poverty without God. What we feel is our need for him,
our, at times, pathetic lack of anything spiritually authentic or real in our life.

It is into this darkness that God comes all filled with
light. It is into our poverty that he returns again and again
without warning so that we might share with him the joy
of rediscovered love. This joy reveals what we desire to
be, not as subject to the half-truths of our superficialities,
but as subject to God's embrace in which an eternal yes
rises from the depths of our inmost Self subsisting in an
indestructible communion with God in his love.

The joy of rediscovered love reveals our need to trust
in God, knowing that what appears to be his absence (as
experienced in what appears to be our poverty) is but his
presence coming to us as a call to deepen our faith in his
ways, which are utterly beyond our understanding. For
God is Presence. There is no absence in him, no distance,
no lack of love, no pulling away. This is what our faith
reveals to us—that even if we would go to the most dis-
tant, most unknown, most forsaken place, he would be
there waiting for us. Even if our sins be as scarlet we are
to trust in him. Even if death itself overtakes us,

"nothing shall separate us from the love of God that comes to us in Christ Jesus our Lord" (Rom 8:38-39). Always he is within us and we in him in an intimate communion beyond anything we can think or imagine.

Thus, when God's apparent absence returns we can by faith move through the mists of appearances to be with God as he is and not as he appears to be. We can know how precious his apparent absence is as the place where he waits for us to meet him. We can listen to the absence, lean into it, learn its ways, dwell in it—waiting, trusting, knowing (with or without consolation, nor in need of any) that God, by this apparent absence, is nurturing the holy desire that is prayer. Thus, too, by a kind of divine serendipity, we discover that in our humble acceptance of our poverty we enter into the first intimations of "the cloud of unknowing" where, like Moses on Mount Sinai, we meet God in the obscurity of contemplation.

Moving from 14th-century England to 16th-century Spain we find in the writings of St. John of the Cross a second source of insight and guidance along the path of intimacy with God in prayer. Like the author of *The Cloud,* he is writing for beginners as well as for those who are more advanced in prayer. In *The Ascent of Mount Carmel,* written explicitly for beginners, he addresses the same basic question addressed by the author of *The Cloud of Unknowing;* namely, How is the beginner to discern whether or not he or she is being called by God to contemplative prayer?

Like the author of *The Cloud* he makes clear that the call to contemplative prayer is a charism received within the context of a genuine Christian life. He counsels the beginner to,

. . . have a habitual desire to imitate Christ in all
your deeds by bringing your life into conformity
with His. You must then study His life in order to
know how to imitate Him and how to behave in all
events as He would (*The Ascent,* Bk. I, chap. 13,
no. 3).*

The imitation of Christ is not carried out from afar,
as though one were imitating the external behavior of a
historical figure. To the contrary, it is carried out within
the context of an intimate bonding with the risen Lord,
who dwells in us through faith. St. John of the Cross
focuses on prayer as that act in which we seek to become
attentive and responsive to the transforming presence of
the Spirit, who achieves this bonding within us and brings
it to perfection.

In Chapter 13 of Book Two of *The Ascent of Mount
Carmel,* the saint provides three signs indicating the call
to abandon a dependence on meditation in order to enter
into contemplative prayer:

The first is the realization that one cannot make
discursive meditation nor receive satisfaction from
it as before. Dryness is now the outcome of fixing
the senses upon subjects which formerly provided
satisfaction. As long as one can, however, make
discursive meditation and draw out satisfaction,
one must not abandon this method (*The Ascent,*
Bk. II, chap. 13, no. 2).

St. John of the Cross has a practical, down-to-earth
approach to questions relating to the practice of contemplative prayer. What we have to do, he advises, is get

---

*All quotes from *The Collected Works of St. John of the Cross*
translated by Kieran Kavanaugh and Otilio Rodriquez. ICS Publications, 2131 Lincoln Road, N.E., Washington, D.C. 20002. 1979.

in touch with what is really going on: Start from where *you* are. Be *yourself*. Pray in the way that it is given *to you* to pray by letting your prayer flow from the reality of *your* life.

For most people this means praying by means of discursive meditation, using thoughts and images. To pray in this way is to pray naturally, for God created us in such a way that we express our loving and being loved through acts, thoughts and feelings of love. Lovers spend many hours talking about a thousand little things, but what is really being communicated in and through their words is their communion with one another in a love no words can express. So, too, when we speak to God in prayer what is of value in his eyes is not so much what we are saying (for what can we possibly tell God that he does not already know infinitely more than we do?). Rather, our words, our thoughts, our imaginings in prayer are precious in his eyes because we are precious in his eyes. We are his beloved. Our prayers are heard by him insofar as they express who we are as created in his image as his chosen one, destined to share in his life forever. Therefore, the more genuine, sincere and self-giving our prayer is the more it unites us to God.

In telling us to practice discursive meditation for as long as possible, the saint is directing our attention beyond all forms of prayer to the one, unutterable love that all heartfelt prayer expresses. It is as though he is saying: Be careful about this contemplation business. It is safer and wiser to turn to God with simple, childlike abandonment to his will and a desire to belong completely to him. It is in forgetting ourselves and our "progress" for the sake of union with God that true progress in prayer begins.

When grounded in this spirit of humble openness to

God, the simple words, "Our Father," or a line from the Psalms become radiant with possibilities. These possibilities have nothing to do with favors that might be bestowed upon us. Rather, the radiance that begins to shine within and around us is that of God awakening us to the truth that he *is* our Father and that we *are* the children of his love.

This radiance is that of faith which shines in the life of every Christian and, indeed, of every child of God. Whatever John of the Cross has to say about the charism of contemplation, his underlying message is that we are to understand that the value of prayer lies solely in its capacity to express and deepen our faith relationship with God in Christ. That is the common legacy uniting all Christians.

But in the text cited above the saint is referring to the Christian who, in getting in touch with where he or she really is, must acknowledge an unexplainable inability to pray using words, thoughts or images. This in itself is a mystery, a sign of God's hidden and mysterious ways. We can pray for the gift of contemplation, but when it actually begins to unfold within us it does so in a form not recognizable as a gift. Rather, it is experienced as a taking away of our own powers that leaves us feeling helpless and confused.

For some, the inability to practice discursive meditation using thoughts and images is dramatic and acute. Like a great door slamming shut, the mysterious obstacle to prayer is experienced as being massive and absolute. For others, it is a much more subtle experience. One is able to pray as before, but an unaccountable sense of emptiness or a vague feeling of dissatisfaction seems to loom over every prayer. Regardless of whether this sense of helplessness in prayer is intense or subtle, the overall effect is the same. It leaves the one who experiences it feeling lost and bewildered and asking, What is happening to me?

This situation calls for some careful discernment. Perhaps the inability to pray as before is due to "one's dissipation and lack of diligence" (*The Ascent,* Bk. II, chap.13, no. 6). Perhaps what is needed is to ask God for the grace to be more faithful in the practice of meditation and its accompanying struggle with distractions and the downward pull of our human frailty. In other words, the first sign, that of the inability to meditate as before, in and of itself is insufficient to determine whether or not one is being called to contemplation. And so the saint continues with a second sign:

> The second sign is an awareness of a disinclination to fix the imagination or sense faculties upon other particular objects, exterior or interior. I am not affirming that the imagination will cease to come and go (even in deep recollection it usually wanders freely), but that the person is disinclined to fix it purposely upon extraneous things (*The Ascent,* Bk. II, chap. 13, no.3).

This second sign is a continuation of the first in that along with the inability to pray by way of thoughts and images, there is a "disinclination" to do so. In fact, this disinclination to focus on thoughts and images is not felt simply with respect to the interior world of prayer, but with respect to external realities as well. While at prayer one experiences an inclination to *stop thinking.* Any "particular," specific thing tends not to hold one's attention.

As the saint makes clear, this does not usually mean that one enters into a trancelike state in which the flow of images ceases to emerge from the ever-active imagination (although sometimes such a cessation of all thoughts and images does occur). What is meant is that none of these images moves one to become "fixed" on what it presents to the mind's eye. Instead, the images tend to flow past like the faces of strangers in a crowd. They move about and all the while something within waits, hopes, yearns for we know not what to appear. In this waiting we come to understand that being distracted in prayer does not mean that thoughts and images continue to appear, but that we waver in the obscure hope that now begins to burn within us.

This is why this second sign must accompany the first. If our inability to use thoughts and images in prayer is not from God, "there is a yearning to dwell upon other things and an inclination to give up meditation" (*The Ascent,* Bk. II, chap. 13, no. 6). That is, unable to focus the mind on thoughts of God one feels drawn to thoughts about things and events in one's daily life. But here, with this second sign, such is not the case. Even though one cannot meditate as before, neither can one find satisfaction on dwelling on other things while at prayer. Every thought, be it religious or secular, be it of interior or external realities, is somehow strangely inadequate and incapable of giving us what we are searching for. Thus, fidelity to daily prayer tends to have the effect of loosening one's grasp upon every finite reference point. One is somehow cut loose and set free upon uncharted, nonconceptual seas. While the desire for prayer remains as strong as ever, it becomes less and less a desire one can understand or talk about. Something is happening deep inside as an undoing that cannot be clearly seen or felt. But it is there nonetheless, moving one irrevocably away from one's attachments and moorings in everything less than God.

St. John of the Cross goes on to point out that these two signs taken by themselves are not sufficient to verify one's call from God to move from meditation to contemplation. The saint, in referring to the inclination not to fix one's mind or imagination on specific thoughts or images, writes, ". . . the cause could be melancholia or some other kind of humor in the heart or brain capable of producing a certain stupefaction and suspension of the sense faculties" (*The Ascent,* Bk. II, chap. 13, no. 6).

The fact that one is inclined to disengage the mind and imagination from all particular concerns, may be due to lethargy, depression, overwork or some other negative influence that undermines the psychic energy required to think clearly, and so a third sign is given:

> The third and surest sign is that a person likes to remain alone in loving awareness of God, without particular considerations, in interior peace and quiet and repose, and without the acts and exercises (at least discursive, those in which one progresses from point to point) of the intellect, memory and will; and that he prefers to remain only in the general, loving awareness and knowledge we mentioned, without any particular knowledge or understanding (*The Ascent,* Bk. II, chap. 13, no. 4).

In each of the first two signs something was taken away. Both the ability to meditate using thoughts and images and one's ability to think in clear, logical terms are removed leaving the impression of being lost in that one no longer understands where one is going. Actually, being in exile might be a more accurate description, in the sense that all attempts to return to former practices and ways of thinking end in failure. One is thus left empty and apparently unable to move forward or to retreat back to safer, more manageable territory. It is into this emptiness that God bestows the "general loving awareness" that is the third and surest sign that one is called to contemplation.

This general, loving awareness is a glimpse of the kingdom within, where God reigns as Lord and master of our lives. Thus, it cannot be compared to anything of this earth. It is the obscure taste of the nuptial emptiness in which we are forever one with God. But since God's loving Presence is also the eternal ground of all that is, everything that is can tell us something of the love from which it springs and upon which it wholly depends. And in this sense, the general loving awareness of God can be likened to the kind of awareness that a man has of the woman he loves. He can look at and be aware of the particular aspects of what he finds to be beautiful in her—the color and texture of her hair, her eyes, the touch of her hand. Or, he can find himself simply being in her presence, in a general, loving awareness of her as the person with whom he is united in love.

This general, loving awareness cannot be produced by any technique. Reading a book titled, *How to Have a General Loving Awareness of the One You Love,* would be of little help. Yet, what he is powerless to achieve by his own efforts is achieved in him by the power of love. It is true he must *choose* to follow love's call. He must freely cooperate with it. But still, it is by love alone that he dwells in her being, that he abides with her in a communion of simple presence.

His general loving awareness does not imply any trancelike state. He still sees her hair, her eyes and all that he saw before, but now the mode of awareness proper to focusing on particular things has been enhanced and somehow transcended by a new awareness born of love.

It is true that this new awareness may, at times, spill over into moments of passion and of other forms of great emotional intensity. At its source, however, it remains more like the air they breathe, like a simple union that surrounds them and makes them one. What can they do but be grateful for and faithful to the gift that has been given?

And so it is with God. In calling us to contemplative prayer he confounds our ability to pray by way of thoughts and feelings in order to draw us with cords of love into a desert of silent waiting where he waits to transform us in the awareness of who we are in him. Sometimes this transforming call to divine union is accompanied by trancelike states. Sometimes there are moments of great emotional intensity or striking intuitive brilliance. At its source, however, the gift of contemplative love is more like the air we breathe. As it opens within us we continue to read the scriptures or to listen to the wind-driven branches tapping against the window. But the mode of awareness proper to focusing on particular things is enhanced and somehow transcended by a new awareness born of divine love that surrounds and sustains us and unites us to God.

St. John of the Cross follows the three signs of being called to contemplative prayer with a clarifying note to the one who experiences them:

> Actually, at the beginning of this state the loving knowledge is almost unnoticeable. There are two reasons for this: first, ordinarily the incipient loving knowledge is extremely subtle and delicate, and almost imperceptible; second, a person who is habituated to the exercise of meditation, which is wholly sensible, hardly perceives or feels this new insensible, purely spiritual experience. This is

especially so when through failure to understand it he does not permit himself any quietude, but strives after the other more sensory experience. Although the interior peace is more abundant, the individual allows no room for its experience and enjoyment.

But the more habituated he becomes to this calm, the deeper his experience of the general, loving knowledge of God will grow. This knowledge is more enjoyable than all other things, because without the soul's labor it affords peace, rest, savor, and delight (*The Ascent,* Bk. II, chap. 13, no. 7).

The saint is not saying that the general loving awareness of God is subtle and delicate at first, but then grows stronger as it develops. To the contrary, he asserts that it is the beginner who must grow stronger in developing a habitual sensitivity to this new, purely spiritual and hence insensible, nonconceptual awareness of God's presence. A habit of quietude and calm must be developed in which the subtle and delicate influx of divine love can establish itself within the life and heart of the beginner.

This habit of learning to resonate with the divine silence cannot be learned by any mechanistic technique on our part, as though we could reach up, grasp the hair of our head and lift ourselves up ego and all into paradise. Nor is such a self-powered attempt at reaching God necessary, for the union we seek with God is eternally achieved in us by God through the prodigal outpouring of his gratuitous love. He always and everywhere draws us to himself, knowing no rest until perfect union is realized.

It seems that the habit we as beginners must cultivate is that of letting God be God by a childlike *faith* in his love as expressed by the simple acceptance of a miracle of grace:

Here I sit, centered in this simple love that I can neither feel nor grasp in an idea. Secretly, it touches me, silences me, claims me. It is not easy sitting thus. I can only move from blunder to blunder, from gift to gift. I am not accustomed to this seeing without thinking, this listening without judgment. I do not know my way in this darkness in which all that is centered in and limited to this "I" I think myself to be senses its own impending demise. And yet, somehow, this way of unknowing, this great death of all that is less than God is simply me being myself in God's presence. It is the way of a self-evident simplicity I cannot see but which nevertheless guides me in everything I do toward an ever-greater intimacy with God. And in this is God's goodness and mercy manifested in my life.

3 THE PRIMACY OF LOVE

When we first begin to practice daily interior prayer we are likely to have some favorite method of prayer, as well as high hopes regarding our progress toward union with God in using it. This is well and good, for we have to begin somewhere, and an enthusiastic hope in making progress is necessary to give us the courage to continue in meditation with the fidelity and determination it requires.

If, however, we sit in silent prayer with a humble heart open to God we will, in ways we know not, be brought to the realization that our imagined goal and the means to reach it must be purified of self-will and all the illusions it engenders if we are to live a genuine life of prayer. This purification is achieved in us by an inner transformation, a *metanoia,* in which we open and abandon ourselves to God's unconditional love. In the art of prayer what has primacy over everything else is to love God in such a way that his love totally claims our life. Above all else, the art of prayer is that of learning to yield to divine love that it might have its way with us.

This primacy of love in prayer is the expression in the silence of our hearts of love's universal primacy in every-

51

day life. Indeed, love precedes life. Whenever a person appears, love is there bringing that person into being. Such a statement seems to fly in the face of the tragic truth that many children are conceived and born into situations opposed to genuine love. But whenever this occurs our innate propensity for love senses the anxiety-ridden unreality arising from love's absence.

A child conceived and born into a world devoid of love is a child still waiting to be born. It is the first touch of real love that brings the child to life. If the lack of love has been intense or prolonged this touch of love may bring birth pangs all its own. How often the source of our sorrow is that we carry within us just such a child. We can, in other words, betray the nature of things, but we cannot alter it, and a fundamental, unalterable truth of life is that our life proceeds from love and without love we cannot endure.

God is the foundation and source of this primacy of love in prayer and daily life. "God is love." Before the beginning, before God said, "Let it be," only love is. This does not suggest a limitation, but affirms that Love is ALL, that He Who Is is Love, that Reality itself is Love itself.

In the beginning, in the mystery of the first love of God's personal creation, God calls us into being to share perfectly in the love he is. Considering a vow to be an act of self-giving love, it can be said that the moment of God's personal creation is a vowed moment in which God gives to us all that he is and waits for us to give to him all that we are. This moment of self-giving love is the ground of every moment. Every moment is, in truth, a vowed moment. Our existence at this moment is the utterance of God's vow to us, his sacred pledge of love that calls us out of nothingness to share in his own divine life. The vowed moment is the moment in which we are, only because we are in him who sustains us in his love. The vowed moment is the real moment. All that is real is so because it comes forth from this moment only to return to the divine secret of its embrace. All that does not come forth from this moment is not real. Everything not of this moment is but a shadow that is passing away. Our awakening to this moment is our discovery of the kingdom of God. It is the fruition of faith and the birth of pure prayer.

The metamorphosis that takes place in this awakening to all that is really real in divine love necessitates the death of a self defined by and limited to the shadows and half-truths which we, in our blindness due to sin, are accustomed to living. Here is the drama of prayer, the journey we did not plan to make that leads us directly to the cross on which everything less than love must die.

It is in prayer that God, in ways unique to each person, leads us along this path that takes us through the crucifixion of our illusions into the realization of the vowed moment in which he eternally unites us to himself in his love. Just how this happens we cannot say. Our inability to explain or understand what God is achieving in us is part of our poverty in which his fullness reigns.

One way of reflecting on this mysterious transformation in love is in terms of options. When we first begin our spiritual journey we have it seems many options in prayer which in turn give rise to many questions. As we travel on, however, the diversity of paths becomes more singular, for the simple reason that our options are taken away. We end up praying in a certain way, not because we have chosen it, but because it is the only way we are able to pray without feeling the strain of artificial and contrived methods that do not apply to us. We are humbled in being reduced to one way we can call our own. We are in this poverty set free as well from the questions arising from options. Our own poverty in God's presence helps clear away the clutter of most misleading and confusing questions.

Then in the detached silence of our waiting even this one way we call our own ceases to be our own as we ourselves become wholly claimed by divine love. It is all very subtle, hardly perceivable, but somehow in the silence we lose our way, somehow there is no way we can call our own. The project we call our spiritual life on which we labored so faithfully, seems to vanish like water poured out onto dry sand as the "I" who prays becomes (we know not how) lost and thereby found in the hidden depths of God's eternal love.

Here, in this moment of losing our way, we begin to realize that the real work of prayer is that of a simple fidelity to a desire established in us by God. The real questions are not those that are answered with explanations but with a love that strengthens us in our weakness and teaches us how not to run away from or do violence to the gentle ache, the quiet hope, the empty bliss that puts to death everything in us that fears and rejects the Father's love. We never thought it would come to this. When we first began our quest we never imagined that love would take up residence in our life, that God himself would become our way by teaching us to let go of everything less than him.

One of the stories told by the Moslem mystics, the Sufis, cautions that a man whose house is too small for elephants should think twice before becoming the best friend of an elephant trainer. He may find himself having to make some unplanned renovations. Similarly, the beginner in the ways of contemplative prayer must not naively imagine that the general loving awareness of God that signals the beginning of contemplation will remain neatly within the boundaries of one's time of daily prayer, for such is not the case. It breaks out at night and rushes into our blood, transforming what was originally thought to be a way to pray into a way of living one's daily life as one claimed by divine love.

What is sown in the silent poverty of wordless prayer blossoms and bears fruit in a daily life in which one comes to recognize the absolute primacy of love in every moment. But what does this mean to live in the awareness of God's loving Presence hidden in the foundations of life itself? As a means of exploring this question, we can turn to the moment in which a man and woman first hear the call to marital love:

When a man falls in love with a woman the love within him calls out to her, becoming the silent, unseen air she breathes. His life is in her hands, for he will live only if she recognizes his love and responds by loving him in return. His very being in this moment is a waiting love that calls out to her.

The love within him knows that he cannot use force. Her freedom must remain intact. And yet, it is now a freedom in which resonates the call to love. She is now someone for whom love waits with unutterable longing.

There is the moment of her awakening to the love that calls her. There is the never-to-be-forgotten instant in which she first looks up into the eyes of love. Before she is ready to receive, before she has even thought of trying to earn it, there is the moment in which she becomes aware she is in the presence of someone calling her to love—what a gift!

Of course the man in this instance is no less the recipient of this gift. There is for him the first moment in which he realizes that a great love has been awakened in him by the presence of this woman. As equals they stand together endowed with a shared awareness of being awakened by the call to love.

By gazing with the eyes of faith into this moment, considered as a primordial sacrament of the divine love that creates it, we can hope to discover a God-given *mandala,* a sacred image in which can be found "hints and guesses" of what it means to live in fidelity to our awakening to divine love. The first lesson that can be drawn from this moment is that of *the need to live in gratitude and openness to moments of love.*

When a man and woman marry they discover soon enough the naiveté of imagining they are going to live in a continual rapture of love. The daily humdrum returns. Their faults remain, but even so they know they have been awakened by a moment of love in which a lifetime of love becomes possible. Their life of love is not an exercise of nostalgia, of continually looking back in remembrance of one moment in the past. Instead, it is an exercise of learning to live in readiness for each new visitation of love:

A man lifts a single strand of hair that has fallen across the face of the beloved. A woman brings in a single rose from the garden as a gift. One cares for the other during a long and serious illness. In these and in countless other ways, love continues to appear in their daily life together. Their growth in love implies a growing sensitivity and responsiveness to these moments in which love's unseen presence unexpectedly appears.

Similarly, a contemplative is someone who has been awakened by the unexpected gift of divine love. As if out of nowhere it appeared, and its appearance has made all the difference, for in love's unexpected awakening a lifetime of love becomes possible. If we look back to the first beginnings of our spiritual journey we invariably come upon moments of spiritual awakening. Sometimes these moments (which appear and reappear throughout our lives) come to us while we are praying. But often they simply rise up out of life itself:

You receive word your father is dying. As you rush to the hospital countless questions and concerns hold you in their grasp. And when you arrive it is as terrible as you imagined. But what you never expected is also true. He says some incredibly simple thing, something funny yet sad, something wise yet childlike. In his hands, clasped upon your own, you become your father's father or mother. And as this child that conceived you slips away over the edge of some great, unseen secret, a vastness opens within you. You walk away silenced and for a moment, wise in the humbling realization that we live out our lives seeing only the tip of the iceberg. And all that does appear above the surface does so only fleetingly as a brief manifestation of some unseen abyss that endows the smallest of things and events with a value beyond comprehension.

Nor are moments of spiritual awakening limited to such awesome events as the death of a loved one. Quite the contrary, moments of awakening are often given to us in life's simplest and most unassuming hour.

Perhaps as a child lying alone at night listening to a summer rain, or in the wake of some unforgivable act when the one we wronged embraced us, or in holding a piece of chipped crystal up to the sun, there was given to us a gift of awareness. (Did we dare even mention it to anyone? Did we dare, even for a moment, to doubt the touch of we-know-not-what that was given there?) Before we did anything to earn it (we can never earn it), before we were ready to receive it (we are never ready), we were granted a gifted awakening.

Such is the awakening of lovers in having been overtaken by an unseen richness that makes everything else to be, by comparison, as nothing. Such is the gifted awakening that makes the artist to be the artist. She or he draws from the Presence, sometimes gently, sometimes fiercely, shapes, sounds, words and colors that enhance our lives. Such is the world in which children live and in which they find their delight. Such is the emptiness around which the very old gather to teeter feebly for a while before falling into its depths.

Thus far the awakening to which we are referring is that of *natural faith* whereby we are able to perceive that the love of God is natural to us, in being the very foundation of our lives. What is significant in a moment of faith's awakening is not the event itself as we weigh its importance in terms of ego consciousness. Nor is the key factor that of the psychological intensity of emotions that may accompany such moments. What is significant relative to a life of interior prayer is the personal realization of having been *awakened* by an inexhaustible vastness, a depth of presence. This awakening, however, is only the beginning, for inherent in the awakening is *the call* to live in fidelity to the depths awakened.

We can, and often do, turn and walk away from such moments as though no awakening had ever occurred. We can go on living in a way that our own experience tells us is not true. That is to say, we can go on living as though all the things we can see, touch, own or control are life itself. We can, that is, sin against the moment of awakening by refusing to be who the moment calls us to be. We can refuse to say yes, and instead con-

tinue to be dominated by superficial levels of consciousness by clinging to the surface appearances of our
life and the world around us. Or, by God's grace we can
choose to be a certain kind of person—someone who
chooses to never betray the Presence.

The gift of *religious faith* does not add anything to
this fundamental option to live in fidelity to life's unseen
depths, for these depths *are* the incarnate ecstasy of
divine love, sustaining us in being and forever calling us
to itself. A religious person, in other words, is not
necessarily more sensitive, humble and open to all that
makes life worth living. In fact, as distorted and falsified
by human weakness, a "very religious person" may be
someone blinded by his or her own religiosity in which an
adamant adherence to biblical texts or dogmas takes the
place of the irreplaceable childlike openness to the divine
mystery of the present moment.

Religious faith, as properly understood and prac-
ticed, does, however, enable us to name the presence as
being the presence of God. As illumined by religious consciousness we can look back to the origins of our spiritual
journey to moments in which we know with an invincible
certitude that we were in the presence of God. Religious
faith endows us with the capacity, and hence the responsibility, to respond to the living God, who has graciously
awakened us to his saving presence in our life.

The gift of *Christian faith* enables us to recognize in
Jesus Christ "the sacrament of the encounter with God"
(Schillebeeckx), the one in whom "the fullness of deity
resides in bodily form" (Col 2:9). As we prayerfully read
the gospels, participate in the liturgy, love others in his
name, we find in Christ a teacher par excellence in learning of the divine presence and how to live in fidelity to it:
"Call the depths Abba," Jesus urges from within. "And

learn from me how not to run away from the advances of his love.''

This, then, is the first insight into living a contemplative life that we would hope to gain from our reflection on the call to marital love; namely, the need to be grateful and responsive to a moment of spiritual awareness. This implies as well the lesson of learning never to rest content in going along with all that tricks us into anxiety over our health, our work, our reputation or any other phenomenon that moves and shifts over the surface of the unseen depths. The lesson offered in a moment of awakening is that of knowing that the hairs of our head are numbered, and that our Abba who knows their number knows as well everything that we need far more perfectly than we could ever imagine. For our heavenly Father knows the one thing necessary is himself as he comes to us in this breath, this heartbeat, this event—waiting to see in us that look of recognition in which we cry, Abba, Father.

This quiet, trusting attentiveness to God's presence will not answer the questions that arise in prayer. But such attentiveness will help us to ask the questions with greater humility and the wisdom of knowing that the pot does not have to understand the gift the potter is drawing forth from its yet-to-be-realized form. The first step toward finding the answer to questions about our spiritual progress is to let go of them in the intuitive awareness that what God is achieving in us is utterly beyond our comprehension. He knows what he is about. And it is enough for us to trust that the God who found no obstacle in our nonexistence in creating us will find no obstacle in our unexpectant ignorance in leading us to perfect union with himself.

As easily as a smile moves across the face of an infant, God moves in us, achieving his will, we know not how. The personal awareness of God's gracious and delicate power as manifested in the spiritual dimensions of our daily life is itself a gift of God. It is the gift of the personal realization that "the fear of the Lord is the beginning of wisdom." And it is as well the beginning of a life of interior prayer.

Returning to the moment in which a man and woman are awakened by the call to love, yet another aspect of the moment can be observed which throws light on the call to contemplative prayer; namely, the call to *intimate communion*. In responding to the call to love, it is not enough that each develops an intuitive sensitivity to love's unseen presence. Nor is the call of love adequately responded to by the cultivation of certain qualities characteristic of a loving man or woman. For the call to love is essentially a call to *intimate communion with the beloved*.

The call to marital love has fire in it. The fire is a shared desire to become unclothed in loving intimacy, such that all one is somehow becomes the beloved's, and all the beloved is somehow becomes one's very self. It is this transubjective unity, this oneness as love makes one that constitutes the sole center and final fulfillment of the call to love.

This same movement toward intimate communion forms the innermost core of our faith. In Christian life it is not enough simply to develop an intuitive sensitivity to God's presence in daily life. Nor is the awakening call to life in Christ adequately responded to by the cultivation of certain loving qualities exemplified by Christ in the gospels. Instead, Christian life is centered in a response of self-giving love in which all that one is somehow becomes God's and all that God is somehow becomes one's very self.

A basic quality of daily consciousness inherent in the call to contemplative prayer is that of a simple desire for a deep, personal, abiding intimacy with God. Whenever one seems to get lost and confused it is often due to losing touch with this childlike yearning for union with God. Reduced to this one primal note, all that constitutes the mystery we call "our life" can be said to originate and culminate in intimacy with God. God creates us moment by moment in the ecstasy of his self-giving love. Our simple "I am" is the outpouring of his very self. And this gift of divine selfhood that is ours in Christ remains unfulfilled until all that I am returns to God to share perfectly in all that he is.

Likewise, all that constitutes the mystery I call my death can be said to originate in my deafness to the divine call to intimacy with God. And all that is known to us as the good news is God's response in Christ to our inability to receive and return his love.

In his journey through our death into the bosom of the Father Jesus turns to us, and with a longing that reaches from end to end, calls out to us saying, "follow me." But who can follow the Lord except the one who, by grace, is willing to die with him to all that fears and rejects the Father's love? And who can die this death except the one who yields to the impulse of the indwelling Spirit of love? This yielding, this following, this dying to all that is less than God is the very essence of prayer, for prayer is the great sacrament of our discipleship in which we follow Christ into the bosom of the Father.

This centrality of the call to personal intimacy with God is the foundation for a common sense, realistic attitude toward the practice of daily prayer. Without a simple desire for personal intimacy with God as one's guide, periods of prayer tend to become dominated by ego concerns over one's technique of prayer and one's progress in perfecting it. In contrast to this, when we sit in prayer as an expression of childlike love, our sitting tends to take on the dimensions of the love that calls us to sit. Our desire for intimacy with God transforms our prayer into a heartfelt attentiveness to God.

When lovers go to be with one another the questions that arise may, on the surface at least, be ego questions: What will I say? How am I to act? But in being together such introspective concerns tend to give way to simply being together. For when they are together in a moment of love everything flows like water. Love takes care of them in showing them there is no how-to-be-with-the-beloved technique against which they can measure their progress in being together. As lovers they simply are *one* in the love that calls them to an ever-greater intimacy.

So too with our meditation. As we are on our way to meditation (and sometimes we can be sitting for a long time and still be on our way), ego questions must be dealt with: Should I kneel or sit cross-legged or lie down? Should I pray the psalms or repeat a mantra? But as we enter into a spirit of attentiveness to God calling us to union with himself such questions tend to give way to a subtle inner communion with God hidden in silence. In this attentiveness of the heart to God's call everything flows like water in our being led by God to the realization that there are no how-to-be-in-the-presence-of-God techniques. A good rule to follow with respect to technique is this: If it helps, do it. If it does not help, do not do it. And here "helps" means simply helps us to forget all concerns over techniques in a simple awareness of God's loving presence and a desire for an ever-deeper union with him. If this means reading the psalms, then read the psalms. If it means to stop reading in order to listen to the rain, then stop reading and listen to the rain.

This pointing beyond all methods and techniques does not, however, mean that diligence is unnecessary in prayer. On the contrary, just as lovers must be diligent in watching over their hearts to detect every infidelity to love's call, so in prayer diligence of the heart is necessary. But again the diligence is not that of the ego employing some kind of diligence-of-the-heart technique. It is rather our humble acknowledgment of every infidelity and our confidence in and gratitude to God who in his mercy continues to call us to himself.

A moment of love between lovers does not flow like water because everything goes well, but because love teaches them to accept one another with all their frailties. Likewise, our prayer does not flow like water because we succeed in avoiding distractions or falling off to sleep or have reached some altered state of consciousness. Rather, our prayer flows like water insofar as it incarnates our inmost Self surrendered over to the flow of God's self-giving love. Our prayer is then our growth into an altered state of consciousness, not at the level at which we enter into a state of trance, but at the foundational level at which we become conscious of God awakening us to his call for us to share in his life. A moment of prayer is a moment of letting go of everything that hinders the transformation that comes with yielding to this call.

The opening pages of the anonymously written 14th-century Christian classic *The Cloud of Unknowing* are devoted to the theme of the primacy of love that underlies the call to contemplative intimacy with God. The author of *The Cloud* begins by telling the beginning contemplative that he has observed that Christian life "seems to pass through four stages of growth" (chap. 1, p. 45).

He labels these four stages as the Common, the Special, the Singular and the Perfect. Each consists of a degree of personal awareness of and transformation in divine love presented in the form of an appeal to the reader's own experience:

> You know yourself that at one time you were caught up in the Common manner of the Christian life in a day-to-day mundane existence along with your friends. But I think that the eternal love of God, which had once created you out of nothing and then redeemed you from Adam's curse through the sacrifice of his blood, could not bear to let you go on living so common a life far from him. And so, with exquisite kindness, he awakened desire within you, and binding it fast with the leash of love's longing, drew you closer to himself into what I have called the more Special manner of living. He called you to be his friend and, in the company of his friends, you learned to live the interior life more perfectly than was possible in the common way (pp. 45-46).

The common manner of living the Christian life refers to what we today would call the cultural Christian. For such a person Christian beliefs and practices fulfill certain psychological needs but without a sense of discipleship, that is, without the personal awareness of being personally loved by God in Christ. In the passage above the author of *The Cloud* describes the transition from this stage to that of a personal awareness of a *special* relationship with God in Christ, and he does so in terms of a divine awakening. Building on this image of an awakening, the beginning of the special manner of living the Christian life can be compared to the experience of being awakened from a deep sleep by a touch of love:

Imagine a man sound asleep. His wife, who has been away for a very long time, returns unexpectedly in the middle of the night, approaches his bed, bends down and awakens him. The awakening is exquisite, not just because it is tender and caring, a gift beyond compare, but because it awakens in him a desire that meets the desire of the one that has awakened him. With the leash of love's longing this desire unites and binds together in a union that gives way to bliss.

God the eternal lover comes to us in the incomprehensible sense of creating us in his image and likeness for himself alone. This moment is his ecstasy. Our life is his rapture, our body the embodiment of his love. Our sin is the ignorance in which as sleepwalkers we move about, not knowing who we really are, for we know not the love that is our life. But the eternal love of God could not bear to see us living in ignorance, walking about in the sleep of unawareness, and so he awakened us to his eternal love for us in Christ. He awakened a desire for him which he has placed within us. Indeed, this desire for God is an expression of our inmost Self, our God-given identity, considered as a capacity to receive, return and enter into the fulfillment of the divine rapture of God's personal creation.

Our personal awakening to this capacity for divine union is our conversion, which has all the excitement of unexpectedly finding a pearl of great price. Our decision to live in fidelity to the discovered gift is our discipleship, which involves all the risk and daring of selling everything we own in order to make the gift our own. Surrendering to the divine gift is our prayer, in which, like the wind that blows where it pleases, God's love stirs in us with exquisite kindness, awakening desires that (in his time and in his way) give way to union.

In calling us to the special manner of living the Christian life God calls us "to be his friend . . . in the company of his friends." The special manner of living the Christian life is a communal life. The disciples in being called to live in union with Jesus were brought into an intimate union with one another. In the book of Acts we read that those whose lives were transformed in the pentecostal fire spontaneously united with those whose lives were also changed in that same fire, and thus was formed the community of the church. Later when cultural Christianity (the common manner of living the Christian life) made it difficult to share a life of discipleship, communities were formed to make this sharing possible. Thus, religious orders and congregations came into existence which gave witness to a life of discipleship through prayer and loving service to others. This same movement toward a communal expression of discipleship can be seen today in every parish which has groups dedicated to Bible study, social justice, or prayer. The institutional church contains the reality of our life in Christ, but it remains for each person to step beyond the structures into that reality, through a life of faith and love expressed in heartfelt prayer and loving service to others.

The author of *The Cloud of Unknowing* introduces the singular manner of living the Christian life by asking, "Is there more?" And to this he responds,

> Yes, for from the beginning I think God's love for you was so great that his heart could not rest satisfied with this. What did he do? Do you not see how gently and how kindly he has drawn you on to the third way of life, the Singular? Yes, you live now at the deep solitary core of your being, learning to direct your loving desire toward the highest and final manner of living which I have called Perfect (p. 46).

The singular manner of living the Christian life refers to the charism of the call to contemplative prayer. Its distinguishing characteristics can be seen in the words used to describe it. The singular manner of living the Christian life is *deep* in that contemplation arises from neither our thoughts of God or our feelings of him, but rather from the depths of God's infinite actuality where he eternally contemplates us in himself. In contemplation one tastes those depths as a divine sweetness and recognizes in it intimations of one's inheritance as a child of God.

The singular manner of living the Christian life is *solitary* in that the depth of the experience of contemplation leaves one alone in the inability to communicate to anyone, including one's self, the mystery of love revealed in it. This deep, solitary core of one's being is where the contemplative lives. Actually it is where we all live. It is where all is one in divine love. But the contemplative is someone called to live in the awareness of this unity, not in a full, conscious sense, but in the obscure sense proper to contemplation.

Finally, in describing the *perfect* phase of Christian life the author of *The Cloud* writes,

> The first three (phases) may, indeed, be begun and completed in this mortal life, but the fourth, though begun here, shall go on without ending in the joy of eternity (p. 45).

The perfect life is perfect precisely because it is God's own life given to us as our deepest Self hidden in him. God creates no other life than our perfect life in union with him. The perfect life is then our real life. It is the life that is.

The phases of Christian life can be seen as an evolutionary development of our awareness of the perfect life that is our true, eternal life in union with God. The *common* Christian recognizes and responds to the perfect life in recognizing, however obliquely, the importance of trying to be a good person, or that religious faith is somehow a value worth preserving. The *special* Christian recognizes the perfect life to be a perfect Someone who shares with us his love and mercy if only we will recognize him and become his disciple. The *singular* Christian recognizes the perfect life as a heartfelt yearning for perfect intimacy and union with God. Addressing himself to the one drawn to this singular intimacy, the author of *The Cloud* cautions:

> . . . mark this. God is a jealous lover. He is at work in your spirit and will tolerate no meddlers. The only other one he needs is you. And all he asks of you is that you fix your love on him and him alone (chap. 2, p. 47).

What are the meddlers that God will not tolerate? A meddler is anything other than your naked self open and responsive to God's touch of love. It is any creature clung to with a heart afraid to die in the emptiness. Thus, in the moment of contemplative union every attachment, every doubt, every fear is a meddler. Everything that causes us to compromise the God-given desire for God is a meddler. This includes a preoccupation with becoming virtuous or becoming a contemplative or becoming anything at all. It includes a sense of discouragement over one's apparent lack of progress in prayer or over some weakness that cannot be uprooted. It includes holding on to any propositional, logical truth about God, be it biblical or otherwise. It includes everything less than the ALL of the eternal love in which we live and move and

have our being and which now touches us, and calls out
to us in the humble darkness of our prayer.

Such love is unmanageable, beyond what we can
bear. The one who experiences its sweet invasions
crisscrossing the sinews of the heart cries out, "How am I
to go on; what am I to do next?" (p. 47).

The author of *The Cloud* responds with an answer
that is radical, simple and profound:

> This is what you are to do: lift your heart up to the
> Lord, with a gentle stirring of love desiring him for
> his own sake and not for his gifts. Center all your
> attention and desire on him and let this be the sole
> concern of your mind and heart. Do all in your
> power to forget everything else, keeping your
> thoughts and desires free from involvement with
> any of God's creatures or their affairs whether in
> general or in particular. Perhaps this will seem like
> an irresponsible attitude, but I tell you, let them all
> be; pay no attention to them (chap. 3, p. 48).

This is what you are to do: Love God. Go to a quiet
place. Calm yourself. And with a gentle stirring of love
lift your heart up to God, loving him not for any of his
gifts, but instead love him for his sake alone. Sitting thus,
do not think about God. Do not turn to take into account
either the absence or the presence of feelings that he is
near. Do not cling to any thought of him, regardless of
how sublime the thought might be. Do not pray for
anyone or for yourself, regardless of the immensity of the
need. Let your love for God for his sake alone be your
sole concern. Of course, you will make mistakes, for,
after all, you do not know what you are doing. You do
not know how to lift up your heart "with a gentle stirring
of love." The very simplicity and radicality of what you

are led to do leads you into the obscurity of the contemplative way. But no matter, led by God's promptings
you learn (without knowing how) to listen to God's gentle
stirrings of love within you. As the gentle stirring is meek,
so, too, is your lifting up of it to God. As it is unseen,
beyond the reach of your power to comprehend it, so,
too, is your lifting up of this stirring. As it is fiery and
mighty, so, too, your humble self-offering to God, loving
him for his own sake.

The author of *The Cloud* goes on to make known the
supreme significance of this heartfelt yielding to divine
love.

> What I am describing here is the contemplative
> work of the spirit. It is this which gives God the
> greatest delight. For when you fix your love on him,
> forgetting all else, the saints and angels rejoice and
> hasten to assist you in every way—though the devils
> will rage and ceaselessly conspire to thwart you.
> Your fellow men are marvelously enriched by this
> work of yours, even if you may not fully under-
> stand how; the souls in purgatory are touched, for
> their suffering is eased by the effects of this work;
> and, of course, your own spirit is purified and
> strengthened by this contemplative work more than
> by all others put together. Yet for all this, when
> God's grace arouses you to enthusiasm, it becomes
> the lightest sort of work there is and one most will-
> ingly done. Without his grace, however, it is very
> difficult and almost, I should say, quite beyond you
> (p. 48).

The first and most important commandment is to
"love God with all your heart, with all your soul, and all
your mind" (Mt 22:37). The contemplative work of the
Spirit is the carrying out of this commandment whereby

you give God the greatest delight. His joy is in knowing this: My child is loving me. My child has discovered why I created persons—that they might be one with me in loving me as I love them.

In this moment of turning to God in detached love all the angels and saints stop, turn to you and listen: Someone is loving God for his own sake. Someone has discovered the love that is eternal life. There is a kind of heavenly rush hour as all the citizens of heaven come to aid you in loving God. You sit alone in him surrounded by all who live in him.

The devils rage over this simple love, for it touches the raw edge of their anguish, which is their refusal and subsequent helplessness to love God. Thus, contemplative prayer involves a wrestling with the powers of darkness, with the realms of spiritual reality within and beyond one's self which are imprisoned in the unreality of being isolated from the ALL of God's love.

Without understanding how, your detached love for God in prayer touches the life of every person on earth. Your childlike fidelity to this simple self-giving love for God carries you in God into his presence in the blood and sinews, the hopes and struggles of each person who lives in the power of his sustaining love. Somehow humanity is your body and the secret joys and sorrows of each person trace lines upon your heart, now given over and surrendered to God in prayer.

The pain of those in purgatory is eased by this simple love. That is, those hidden in the mystery of purification after death are somehow touched by this simple love for God. And, of course, you, too, are enriched by the work of the Spirit more than all others put together. Whatever is done *for* God is somehow gathered together in this silent, heartfelt being with God. All that enriches, all that has value, all that fulfills is somehow dependent upon this great letting go of self, this childlike surrender to the loving communion with God to which you are called.

Reading this passage of *The Cloud* and reflecting upon it can be compared to standing in a Gothic cathedral looking up into an intricately faceted rose window that casts a bluish ethereal light on the carved images of saints, demons and angels. If one so chooses, all can be dismissed as medieval naiveté, hardly worth a moment's serious consideration. Or one can sit awhile and try to appreciate and get in touch with this spiritual vision so different from ours today. Or one can simply pray and thereby enter into the divine presence that stirred the hearts of those who built this expression of their faith in God.

Similarly, the above passage taken from *The Cloud* can be read as being nothing more than a collection of quaint medieval images. It can be read as a vision of reality that one would not want to take seriously, except, perhaps, to use as an example of medieval distortions of the gospel or lack of awareness of social justice and other vital concerns. Or one can read the passage with a sense of appreciation for the beauty and wealth of religious intuition it expresses and which forms part of the heritage of the church.

While the latter of these two responses to the text expresses an admirable sensitivity, it is nonetheless tangential to the one response that carries us beyond the surface structures to the timeless message that is being conveyed: Fix your love on God, forgetting all else. Taste for yourself the mystery of the kingdom of God—the mystery of God enraptured and lost in us as awakened to and lost in him.

This response is a grace. When aroused by grace the

simple letting go, the yielding of self in silence, is the lightest sort of work there is. As one turns to one's lover in the darkness, or as a child abandons itself in its father's arms, we, in response to God's grace, intuitively open ourselves to God's transforming embrace. Without grace, however, this is impossible. We remain, as it were, trapped in our thoughts, our feelings, our questions and answers, unable to go beyond ourselves into God. In the moments of grace we come to know of God's goodness. In the moments we are left to our own devices we come to know of our need for God's saving mercy

This third chapter ends with a plea for the beginning contemplative to "learn to be at home in this darkness" in which one waits for God in expectant silence. Home is where one was born, and thus this silence is our home, it is the return to our point of origin in God's love. Home is where one belongs, and thus this silence is our home, for we know God wills us to be here in this waiting. If we get up and walk away we become exiled from our own deepest truth in God. And home is where we live, thus this silence is our home for we live here in this waiting for God. Throughout the day there are flashes of desire, glimpses of the beloved, intuitions of the Presence that reveal that we are grounded in this simple love no matter where we go or what it is we might be doing.

This journey into radical, transcendent love is at times arduous. Dying to self is never easy. But the author of *The Cloud* ends with a word of encouragement, telling the beginning contemplative:

> If you strive to fix your love on him forgetting all else, which is the work of contemplation I have urged you to begin, I am confident that God in his goodness will bring you to a deep experience of himself (p. 49).

4 SOLITUDE

There is something innately solitary about living a life given over to contemplative intimacy with God. This comes as no surprise. There is something innately solitary about life. And the student, the artist, anyone engaged in an enterprise of drawing upon life's hidden resources will, at times, feel the need to be alone in order to deepen consciousness, to get in touch with levels of awareness that can easily become lost in the day-by-day shuffle of continually being in the presence of others. Similarly, those attempting to practice daily meditation will instinctively rise early in the morning or find some other oasis of silence during the day in order to be alone in prayer.

To be alone is to expose one's self to feelings of loneliness and isolation from others. Part of a life of prayer consists in learning how not to be afraid of the pain of loneliness, but instead to endure it patiently, learning from it invaluable lessons in self-knowledge. But this inevitable and potentially positive dimension of loneliness must not lead one to equate solitude with physical isolation and feelings of loneliness.

Feelings of isolation are associated with a sense of

personal impotence, a helplessness to communicate with others in an effective and productive way. Solitude, on the other hand (while involving feelings of isolation and the truth they contain), is more properly associated with a sensitivity to the interior depths of our being, in which we subsist in a profound, unseen unity with all that is. A scholar in his or her many hours alone may experience acute feelings of loneliness. But these are overshadowed by (but not necessarily removed by) the excitement and the intensity of the pursuit of truth. An artist knows very well what loneliness is, but this is nothing compared to the intuitive illuminations that constitute the creative moment. Solitude is then a *relational term,* referring to the quality of our awareness of our relationship with all that lies within and which gives meaning and purpose to our lives.

The felt need to be alone in order to pray can, in part, be attributed to the need to deepen consciousness of the interior, spiritual dimensions of our being. Most people find that some degree of physical solitude is helpful in fostering the interior silence required to penetrate to the living center of a text of scripture or to sit in a way that offers the least resistance to the subtle and delicate movements of interior prayer.

But these psychological considerations are in themselves inadequate in serving as a basis for an understanding of the true nature of solitude as expressed in interior prayer. For while the solitary nature of prayer embraces the whole of our being, including the psychological, it also transcends our being in bringing us into an encounter with the living God. Or, more precisely stated, it brings us to the transforming awakening of the relationship with God in Christ which *we are* and are forever destined to be.

Phrased differently, solitary prayer is essentially an act of *religious faith,* and therefore can be adequately appreciated only in terms of our relationship with God in Christ, which faith and prayer express. The solitary nature of prayer is then not determined by whether or not one happens to be physically alone or with others. Nor is it determined by any state of mind, in the sense that one is more solitary while absorbed in meditation than when absorbed in the routines of ordinary daily life. For solitude is ultimately determined by God alone, who in creating us in his image and likeness, calls us to a *relationship* with himself that makes us to be sharers in the eternal, perfect solitude of Christ the Word.

Christ the Word is eternally alone in being the only one who is, by nature, perfectly one with the Father in the unity of the Holy Spirit. In creating us in the eternal image of this unity, the Father calls us to be one with him as Christ is one with him. He calls us to the eternal solitude of being so one with him in Christ that God is left alone in us and we in him in the unity of God's trinitarian love.

When Jesus, the historical Christ, spent whole nights alone in prayer he was no doubt restoring the vital energy that was being continually poured out in his daily relationships with others. But more than this, he was being faithful to who he is as the one who says, "I and the Father are one" (Jn 10:30). In his hours of solitary prayer Jesus was being faithful to his perfectly unique and therefore perfectly solitary union with the Father. When he returned to his disciples and spoke to them he did so out of this union and with no other ultimate end than to awaken us to our call to share in that union forever.

Jesus instructs us, his disciples, in how we are to pray: "When you pray, go into your room and shut the door and pray to your Father who is in secret; and your

Father who sees in secret will reward you" (Mt 6:6). We can see here a warning against the hypocrisy of praying to win the admiration of others. We can see, too, an invitation to enter into the secret place of that unique and therefore solitary intimacy with God that is our innermost Self created by the Father through Christ the Word. This place is secret because it bears no admittance to a dualistic observer. It permits not the companionship of an "other." It is the place of uniqueness in unity, the place in which we say in all truth, "For me to live *is* Christ."

The God-given metaphor of marital love provides a point of insight into the nature of our solitary intimacy with God and how it is experienced in the poverty of heartfelt prayer. The beloved stands before me as one who proclaims: "You and only you are the one I love. Only you in all of creation can fulfill my desires for fulfillment in love by accepting my love and loving me in return."

In standing thus in the presence of the beloved I am in solitude first with respect to myself. That is, at the level of consciousness at which I perceive myself to be one among many I cannot grasp with my own mind my uniqueness in the beloved's eyes. For here, in this moment, I am awakened to the beloved calling me to realize *there simply are no others.* Unable to comprehend with my own mind this solitary uniqueness in which I stand alone, filling the horizon of the beloved's being, I am called by love to make an act of *faith.* I am called by the truth of the moment to accept in faith who the beloved calls me to be in love. By this act of faith I enter into my solitude in accepting my unique relationship of loving intimacy with the beloved in whose eyes I catch glimpses of a Self-in-love, which I cannot see but which I am asked simply to be.

By the same token, my power to name the beloved also leaves me in solitude with respect to myself. Accepting my responsibility to unveil the uniqueness of the beloved by calling her or him to love reveals my own uniqueness as well. In the moment my call to love awakens the beloved, her or his eyes fall upon me alone. I stand alone before the one who stands alone in my love. Thus, in both calling and being called, *love reveals that solitude arises from one's incommunicable uniqueness in the presence of the beloved.* And this uniqueness leaves me in solitude with respect to myself in that what I know so clearly as an *experience* remains unknown, and in a certain sense unknowable to me as an object of conceptual inquiry. The knowledge given in love is always in some sense a knowledge that is received secretly, from within, in ways hidden in solitude.

This solitary dimension of love has its principle in God. To be awakened by the call of faith is to sense something of my incommunicable uniqueness in God's eyes. So perfectly unique is my relationship with God that I myself cannot understand it. Thus, left in solitude with respect to myself, unable to grasp with my own mind the union to which I am called, I can only be who faith calls me to be. I can only, with God's grace, surrender to the divine intimacy that is the life of my innermost Self hidden with Christ in God. And this surrender is my prayer.

So solitary is the secret place of prayer that I cannot even take myself along. So singular is the unity to which I am called that I must make the journey without the companionship of the ego-self that makes observations of my progress. The self that decides, judges, that loses track of itself and rediscovers itself must be abandoned as the basis out of which I hope to advance in prayer. For in its dualistic consciousness of itself it cannot enter into that perfect mutual self-emptying unity with God in Christ that is the Self fashioned in the image of God's ecstatic love.

The love of God is the only basis that can support a life of interior prayer. And it is this foundation of divine love—known so intimately in the depths of faith—that leaves me so alone in the inability of my external consciousness to understand it.

Here is the paradox of solitude: My inmost self is in solitude with God by virtue of being itself a relationship of likeness to him in his love. I am *one* with God as love makes one. I am hidden in him and he in me in the perfect unity of his ecstatic love. And by this very unity (that is the Self) I, in my external ego consciousness, am left alone. For I am left without any tangible evidence that appears on the limited terms available to the ego that would prove to "myself" that this unfolding intimacy with God in prayer is, in fact, real.

I can see evidence of it in my life. A peace, a wholeness, a sense of genuineness may be noted with unmistakable certainty. But the root source, the core of this qualitative personal growth remains hidden. If I sit in prayer with a humble heart open to God I eventually reach a point beyond which my grasp of my own journey must be left behind. Eventually I reach the point of solitude in which I am asked to sit in prayer without the ability to understand, to justify or to explain to anyone or to myself where I am going and how I am getting there.

Solitude is not entered into by way of subtle introspections. The ego self does not transcend itself by its own efforts at self-transcendence. Solitude is entered in the pure simplicity of divine love. Perhaps with a great deal of emotional fervor or perhaps in a dry-as-dust subtle stillness God awakens me to his love in a way that is utterly personal and existential.

In the solitude of this awakening I spontaneously cry out in silence—God loves me so! He touches me with his beauty. He moves in me awakening desires for him that I cannot contain nor hope to fulfill unless he fulfills them in me. So deep is this awakening to his love that it is what I know most deeply. And yet its very depth makes it to be what I do not know at all. When God touches me I cannot speak. I cannot put one idea up against another. To attempt to explain, to justify, or even to look at—all fill me with a sense of shame as well as a sense of my own foolishness.

And in this I am left in solitude with respect to myself: I must now have *faith* in this love that touches me so deeply as to transcend me, leaving me, as it were, hanging in midair unable to find any footing except in the unseen love that keeps drawing me beyond myself into a union with God I cannot understand.

The more I advance in my fidelity to my solitary intimacy with God in prayer, the more I come to realize that it is not enough that I spend so much time each day in prayer. What God asks of me is an abiding faith in him in which, by his grace, I pass alone beyond a point of no return into a solitary center where he waits for me to give myself to him forever as he gives himself to me. What he asks of me in prayer is that I trust him enough to let go of my dependency on everything less than him, so that he can lead me in incommunicable poverty into the fullness of his love. He asks that I accept who I am in the depths that open beneath my feet in the moment when Silence cloaks me in itself, revealing that I am forever one with God. And he asks that I have faith in him in the hour of shadows when temptation, failure or discouragement seem to hold me in their power. He asks, that is, that I live in solitude with respect to myself in going forth from myself into a union with him that is hidden in faith.

The experience of being in solitude with respect to myself corresponds to the experience of being in solitude with respect to *others*. In following God's call into solitary prayer I am led not simply beyond my own understanding, but beyond the understanding of others as well. God draws me with cords of love into a desert no one can find except the Self I am hidden in him. Here in this desert of his own infinite actuality he tells me of his love in a language unknown to all save himself and the Self fashioned in the image of his love. Thus, the more clearly I hear his voice calling me to union, the more clearly I am alone with God in solitude with respect to both myself and others.

A clarification of the nature of solitude with respect to others is provided by Rainer Maria Rilke in the book, *Letters to a Young Poet* (W.W. Norton, 1934). In this work of collected letters Rilke responds to a young poet who has sent Rilke some poems he had written, asking Rilke to tell him whether or not his poems were any good. In response to his request, Rilke writes:

> You ask whether your verses are good. You ask me. You have asked others before. You send them to magazines. You compare them to other poems. . . . I beg you to give up all of that. You are looking outward, and that above all else you should not do now. Nobody can counsel and help you, nobody. There is only one single way. Go into yourself. Search for the reason that bids you to write; find out whether it is spreading out its roots in the deepest places of your heart, acknowledge to yourself whether you would have to die if it were denied you to write. This above all else—ask yourself in the stillest hour of your night: must I

write? Delve into yourself for a deep answer. And if this should be affirmative, if you may meet this earnest question with a strong and simple, "I must," then build your life according to this necessity; your life even in its most indifferent and slightest hour must be a sign of this urge and a testimony to it (pp. 18-19).

In the above passage Rilke is not attempting to dull the young poet's search for guidance. On the contrary, he is guiding the young poet to the point of realizing that no other human being can provide the guidance that comes only from within. He is, in effect, telling the young poet that while remaining open to everyone who may have something to offer, he must, at the same time, appreciate the fact that this openness to others will lead to a crippling dependency and loss of spiritual integrity unless he is also open to the innermost recesses of his being where the creative impulse lies hidden.

The question, Are my poems any good? has connotations of the ego-self seeking to affirm itself in the approval of some authority figure. But the question, Must I write? denotes instead a person who has deepened consciousness in the stillest hour of the night. It is the question of someone willing to risk facing the inner imperatives of his or her own spiritual truth.

Similarly, in prayer it is vitally important to remain open to whatever guidance others might be able to give. But this openness to others will be of little real benefit unless we face our own inner imperatives in the presence of God by asking, Must I pray?

This "must" is not such that it robs me of my freedom. I am still free to pray or not to pray. But the inner necessity of prayer is such that I must pray if I am to be the person I know in my heart that God is calling me to be. My fidelity to daily meditation is then my free acceptance of God's call to intimacy with himself. It is my free decision to live in Christ in the way the Spirit is calling me to live in him.

The must of prayer is its solitude. It is the point at which I *must* cease leaning upon the understanding or approval of anyone, including myself, by simply accepting the inner imperative that claims me for itself as someone who must pray.

Thus, the fundamental question of prayer is not among the questions that can properly be directed outward to another, such as, "Am I praying in a manner best suited to my present needs?" or "How can I learn to deal effectively with distractions?" Nor am I myself qualified to answer the fundamental question of prayer in the sense that I can be my own source of spiritual wisdom. The fundamental question of prayer can be answered by God alone: Why do I pray? Because I must pray. How do I know I must pray? Who told me? No one told me. I know because I have listened in the stillest hour of the night to the inner promptings of my heart which I know by faith to originate in God moving me to seek him in prayer. It is at this point that prayer is interchangeable with love. For now prayer is no longer simply an act of communication with God, but is rather one's yielding to the solitary recognition of being at one with God in his love. This communion is not of this earth. It is of God in his will for us to be one with him.

What contributes to one's solitude with respect to others is the all-pervasive nature of one's incommunicable intimacy with God in Christ. The inability to communicate to another the solitary taproot of prayer is intensified by the inner dynamism of God's love which begins to manifest itself in our slightest hour, in our every vulnerability to love catching us off guard simply being who we are:

A man goes out into the back yard at night, perhaps to close a gate that one of the children had left open. Turning to walk back to the house he looks up, and through the window sees his wife sitting in the living room, reading a book to one of their children. He stands there for a fleeting moment in a darkness illumined by a spontaneous contemplation of love. He glances up into the vastness of the stars and life begins all over again in a beauty "ever ancient, ever new."

Every time we sleep the contemplative awakens wearing robes of archetypal fire . . . everytime the beautiful snags us and holds us momentarily in its embrace . . . in every instance where the presence of a loved one overflows the banks of the explainable . . . or our own solitude awakens in a desert where we stand naked alone in the divine presence—in such moments we know (without knowing) that God is, that we belong to him, and that, although in this life we will never understand how, God is forever drawing us to himself.

Turning once again to the artist as exemplifying this solitary consciousness, a woman sits alone painting a landscape. As she works her perceptions shift and deepen. The eyes of the artist open within her, revealing hues and colors not seen before. It is from this depth of aesthetic awareness that she picks up her brush to paint. Who in that moment can tell her what to do? No one can say a word, nor can she herself intervene to manipulate the gifted, unguarded moment of the creative act. Yet how closely this unguarded moment (unseen and unknown in its origins) must be guarded! With what discipline must she form her life according to what it asks of her! In the creative moment she loses her way and enters into the way of her giftedness. When she simply acts in fidelity to the gift given, all is clear and self-evident. When, however, she attempts to explain to herself in logical terms how this happens she cannot do so. When she turns to another to explain the inner movements of the creative act, it is then she realizes her solitude with respect to others. She cannot explain to others what is most immediate, most basic to her way of being in the world.

The practice of contemplative prayer in its externals is simply the preparatory ritual that provides entrance into the unguarded moment in which the heart lies open and responsive to God's art in us. And yet how carefully this unguarded moment, once realized, must be guarded! How quickly conquests and defeats, obstacles and goals, questions and answers return to reclaim us and make us once again their servant. And yet with the unforced reverence of a child at play, we, by God's grace, can sit in fidelity to the Presence that never appears but which, with a sweet unseen fire, names us as a child of the Father. We cannot contain nor manage this life in which little by little we become lost in God. We cannot comprehend this union with God that springs from deep within where our thoughts and feelings cannot reach.

Small wonder then that no one else can understand it either. Small wonder that no other human being can understand the transformations that God is achieving within us. At the level of ego consciousness this inability of others to understand our most intimate relationship with God can be painful. It is only natural to want a best friend or one's spouse to share the inner journey toward God. In fact, to the extent I have yet to die to my ego existence as the basis out of which I am attempting to live a life of prayer, I will experience my solitude with respect to others to be nothing more than this painful incommunicability.

However, as I learn to accept this incommunicability I can discover in it a divine gift. In being unable to understand the intimacy with God that is the center of my life, others give me the gift of solitude! By being unable to enter into the sanctuary of my inmost self one with God, others give witness to the truth that although surrounded by others I am alone with God.

The painful aspects of feeling there is no one who understands is alleviated somewhat by the good fortune of having a spiritual director. A good spiritual director is someone who does possess a true understanding of this journey toward contemplative intimacy with God. This understanding, however (arising from the director's own fidelity to the inner way), is grounded in the director's awareness that he or she dare not interfere with God's work. A good director can help to avoid some of the tangents and pitfalls along the way. He or she can give witness to the Reality of what one is seeking. But the advice and encouragement are given in a manner that clearly avoids giving answers that would dispel one's sense of being in solitude with God. Instead, the loving encouragement of the director seems only to intensify one's awareness of being, in some mysterious way, alone with God, beyond human help.

With or without the benefit of a director, one arrives eventually at a graced realization of the paradox of solitude in relation to others. The paradox is this: As I die to ego consciousness in fidelity to humble prayer, I discover my incommunicable intimacy with God is actually the ground of my incommunicable intimacy with others. As I grow in the awareness of who I am, one with God in his love that sustains me, I grow, too, in the awareness of who I am as one with others in that self-same love:

A mother is at home trying to pray while her small child is playing on the floor near her feet. The child's constant movements, its requests to be helped now with this toy, now with another, are a continual distraction to her. At the level of ego consciousness the child is an obstacle to her attempts to recollect herself in prayer.

But then, by God's grace, she looks at the child in solitude, she sees the child through the eyes of the love that impels her to pray. Is it that her awareness of the child incarnates the divine awareness in which God eternally beholds the child in the depths of his unfathomable love? Is it that in this moment she is given to realize that this child incarnates all that Christ is? She cannot say. But for a moment she gazes at her child, and this simple gaze of love becomes her prayer. It is in eternity that she repents of her blindness in reaching out to touch the child's face. It is with humility that she acknowledges her foolishness in seeing only an obstacle to God, in this child so fraught with the divine. For in this vowed moment the beauty of the child's presence touches her, wounds her, silences her with the beauty of God's presence. And in this bonding with her child in the love of God, prayer spontaneously stirs within her.

This spiritual awareness of our unity with others in divine love does not awaken in us simply while we are praying. On the contrary, it unexpectedly manifests itself as being the hidden ground supporting every encounter with another:

You are visiting a nursing home when, without warning, a depth of divine presence calls out to you from the face of a feeble man. In obedience to this call you sit with this man as you would with a friend that you have known for a very long time. You laugh with him in the simplicity of his wisdom, which he cannot articulate, which he himself cannot see, but which radiates from him simply being who he is.

You are given the privilege of an unexpected visit from a friend who is mentally handicapped. She is special to you not because she is "different" but rather because in being different she helps you to realize how much the two of you are alike: You, too, are limited in countless ways. You, too, are able to utilize but a fraction of your potential. You, too, fail to make the most of the connections. And you, too, are a person bestowed with a value that you will never completely know until you are dead. Touched by these intuitive convictions, you sit with her eye to eye, talking, sharing, simply being with her—grateful for her presence.

The circumference of one's discovered union with others in the solitary intimacy of divine love has a way of widening out to include everyone. Indeed, the desert of solitary transformation in divine love is the origin of prophetic speech. Words that come from one's silent communion with God are words that have the power to move the hearts of others. Actions that incarnate the compassion that one breathes in prayer are prophetic actions that have the power to give witness to the presence of the kingdom on earth. The more genuinely one lives in solitude with God, the more clearly one sees that social justice is not an issue but a metaphysical necessity.

Perhaps in the beginning of our spiritual journey we placed an emphasis on the difference between daily activities with others and our times alone in prayer. It is true that no amount of prayer can ever take the place of loving and being loved by others, just as loving and being loved by others cannot take the place of prayer. At the same time, however, we discover that in fidelity to prayer and loving and being loved by others, the lines of demarcation between these two spheres break down. The union with God we seek in prayer embraces us unexpectedly in a moment of simply being with another person. And in a moment of solitary prayer we are granted a sudden awareness of another with a heightened capacity to love that person, to accept him or her in the compassion that holds us in our prayer.

While at one level remaining quite distinct, the experience of sitting in meditation and the experience of being with others come together as two manifestations of one divine call—to say yes to each new, unexpected manifestation of love. Always the movement is the same—yielding again and again to the freedom of the eternal Someone who forever calls us to himself, now in this moment of silent prayer, now in this moment with others. Without knowing how, being with others and being alone in prayer empty into one another as two manifestations of the call to be with God. Both the silence of our prayer and the nearest thou at hand lure us into an ever more faithful following of the divine call to die to ourselves so as to be born into the Love that is our life.

5 TO KNOW GOD

The contemplative journey most often begins not by setting out one day to become a contemplative, but by entering into the hidden center of prayer to discover God uniting us to himself in the obscurity of faith. One prays the psalms and discovers there a transparent joy not known before. One slowly recites the Our Father and senses in the words the Father's presence. One receives the Eucharist and tastes the sweetness of love incarnate. Such moments are, or should be, known to all Christians as a natural consequence and source of faith. Deep within, God abides in a perfect communion with our innermost Self hidden in him. In moments of prayer the divine bliss of this union rises up into ego consciousness as a faint tremor of the divine presence.

Those called to contemplative prayer find that these touches of divine love create a need. They make one aware of a subtle, pervading inadequacy that can be remedied only by finding a more abiding personal realization of intimacy with God. And so drawn by the imperatives of love unfulfilled one goes to one's room, closes the door and seeks the Father whose indwelling

Spirit has awakened one's inner being to his call to union with himself in Christ. As instinctively as an animal in the desert finds water, the inner self seeks out that prayerful surrender in which one sits, grows silent, faces the emptiness of faith's unseen hope and waits.

It is all very awkward at first trying to maintain one's balance riding on an unalterable desire. When, however, this silent attentiveness to the divine presence is accepted with childlike faith it is the most natural of acts. It is, in fact, simply our humanity being itself in fulfilling the purpose for which God creates it; namely, to be the means through which we seek union with him.

The one who sits is the one who knows. In our sitting in contemplative stillness we give up our own will and thereby come to know God as he wills us to be one with him in his love. We give up our dependency on thoughts and images, our knowing God on our terms, and thereby enter into a graced unknowing, a being with God as he knows us in himself before he said, "Let it be." But what does it mean to say such things? What is the nature of this awakening of Christ consciousness? What is this enlightenment that shines forth in the darkness of contemplative love?

St. Thomas Aquinas, St. Teresa of Avila and others wrote of the *purgative, illuminative* and *unitive* ways as three stages of perfection of charity and purification from sin through which the soul passes in its journey toward union with God. By adapting the meaning of these terms to apply specifically to stages of faith awareness of the living God, we can explore some of the characteristics of contemplative wisdom in which one obscurely knows God as he is in himself.

The purgative way is the way of salvation. That is, it is knowledge of God given in an existential encounter with the mystery of the cross. To see what this means in this context we begin with a passage taken from the gospel according to St. Mark:

> People were bringing little children to him, for him to touch them. The disciples turned them away, but when Jesus saw this he was indignant and said to them, "Let the little children come to me; do not stop them; for it is to such as these that the kingdom of God belongs. I tell you solemnly, anyone who does not welcome the kingdom of God like a little child will never enter it" (Mk 10:13-15).

How does a little child accept the kingdom? Not by a design of his or her own making, but rather by simply be-ing a child:

A father scoops his infant child up into his arms and in doing so is himself caught up in a moment of boundless love. The child in this moment cannot perform a single act to acquire the father's love. For one cannot acquire what is already given. And what is given here is not in the order of possessions attained through actions, but of love received through the pure gratuity of love. The child in this moment is doing nothing. It is simply be-ing the child the father loves. This is enough. This is everything.

The child rests in a profound obedience, a simple, unself-aware be-ing in the arms of the one who conceived it and who now bestows upon it the gift of his love. Since there is no action here save that of the father's love, there is no shadow cast upon his love, no dualistic obstacle presented to it. There is in the child no one other than one held and possessed by love.

Ego has not yet awakened in the child. There is as yet no center of consciousness to give birth to an act with a purpose of its own. Hence, the child's actions are non-

actions, leaving no trace of an "I" that calls an action "mine." This egolessness does not call into question the value of the child as a person, but rather points the way to the realization that the child's identity as a person is revealed in the love that now shines in the father's eyes. The child's true face is reflected there as one who is worthy of all love has to offer.

God is our Abba, and we are the children of his love. This is enough. This is everything. This is the truth of who we really are in him who is our life. We, however, do not perceive ourselves as such. We do not live in the awareness of the unity with God that is our innermost Self conceived in his love. Instead, we tend to experience ourselves as being a separate, autonomous ego. This is the original sin, the original ignorance and from it comes all our pain and suffering. This is the great illusion that makes everything I see to be ultimately false in that the vantage point from which I observe everything (my own autonomous ego) is itself false and unreal.

As the victim of this falsity and illusion I am thinking, always thinking, maintaining myself in existence by maintaining my ideas of myself, of others and of everything around me. I have thoughts too of God and of how to reach him. I open my Bible, quoting now this verse, now that one. I observe my behavior and the behavior of others. I take notes. I sort out the chaff from the wheat, weighing everything in the scales of my judgment or the judgment of some group to which I have identified myself and consider myself a member.

God in his goodness reveals to me the ultimate unreality of this entire process which in my ignorance I would call my life. In one moment of genuine religious experience he opens my eyes to the truth. He touches me with an intuitive awakening of his presence. He pierces me with a single glance of his love. He bows down through the clouds of my oblivion, picks me up in a moment in which every thought is silenced, every opinion put to rest, every shadow of an illusory separate self dispersed in the eternal light of the truth he utters within me: You are the child of my love. My life is yours and your life is mine. Our unity is who you are.

This is a taste of the great deliverance, the good news of divine childhood. By authentic religious experience, initiated by God revealing himself to me, I am brought into an existential awareness of an identity hidden with Christ in God which transcends the boundaries of my contingent ego self. This is a source of deep spiritual joy and peace, to know by my own experience that I am not simply this observable self caught in the vicissitudes of life's changing circumstances. I am a spiritual self, a relation of likeness to God in his love, one entitled by his birthright to cry, "Abba, Father."

But, of course, it is not as easy as this. To the extent I am attached to my illusions of myself as being nothing more than ego, this good news appears before me as the cross upon which the self sustained in these illusions must die.

We need not try to find the cross but only to stop running from it. This is what contemplation entails—the cessation of the flight from God. Actually, even in contemplative prayer's most sublime moment, the flight continues. We cannot help it. But we can with God's grace express the desire to be overtaken by God in our flight from him.

The hawk and sparrow meet in midair, who knows the ritual enacted there? No one. Even less can anyone grasp the paradoxical gift given by God to the one he overtakes in silence. As if in midair the self sustained in gains and losses, sins and virtues is revealed to be but a vapor. The great deliverance is the great death to the self of separateness, for the gift given is received into the sweet, enigmatic undoing of who we thought ourselves to be.

We need not seek a method to achieve this. Indeed, it is the giftedness that begins to arise where methods and the self sustained by them leave off. We need only to sit. The silence itself will show us the way. The sitting itself is the way—the incarnation of our waiting.

It would be foolhardy and quite impossible to force one's way into this naked poverty. What one needs to do is to continue praying each day as it is given to one to pray. In God's time and in God's way the gift of undoing begins. In between the words the subtle aura of stillness begins to purge us of our understanding by instructing the inner heart in the ways of love.

To sit thus is not simply to know that Christ died for us or to have feelings of love for him in gratitude for his saving death. It is instead a sharing in the cross by an existential self-emptying in love that begins the moment we become silent and still enough to experience it and yield to its paradoxical richness.

In a quiet breathing of love a knowledge is given that is to the ego as no knowledge at all. The crucified mind knows God without knowing anything. As the ego sleeps the inscape of love unfolds within a heart hidden in faith. Only by its fruits is it known—an innermost thirst for God and a greater capacity to love and be loved by others. But in turning to know what one knows, in wanting to possess it in a clear idea or feeling, it vanishes in the betrayal of the unity in which it is received. This knowledge is not given to a separate self that grasps and possesses, but to a surrendered self that waits, yields and is transformed.

The illuminative way is the way of creation. It is the knowledge of one's self and of all that is as proceeding from an act of God's creative love. As blinded by our attachments we tend to see ourselves and all that is around us in relation to our needs. As we are purified of our attachments we begin to see in a new, more authentic way by intuiting the *being,* the reality of ourselves and all that is in our relationship, not to our needs but to God creating us moment by moment for himself alone.

This, in fact, is the purpose of salvation, to restore us to the first love of God's personal creation. Relative to the mystery of our ignorance due to sin the text "God loved the world so much that he gave his only Son" (Jn 3:16) refers to our redemption. But relative to the mystery of who the Father calls us to be in Christ this text refers to our creation. God loved the world so much that he gave his only Son in the radical, ontological sense of calling us to share in his life as the Son shares in that life. This is Christ's prayer, that we might be one with the Father *even as* he and the Father are one (Jn 17:21).

Christian contemplative prayer draws its vitality from a personal participation in the death and resurrection of Jesus. Thus, a personal devotion to the humanity of Christ in his saving work of redemption is fundamental to a life of interior prayer. But as this participation bears fruit in our lives, as we die with Christ in the emptiness, we begin to realize the fruition of salvation—a mystical identification with the person of the Word, through whom we subsist as called to perfect union with God.

As we are delivered from the ignorance that holds us captive in what we are not and never can be (a separate self apart from God), we are born into the awareness in which we cry Abba-Father. As the illusion dies, the reality emerges. As the self born in disobedience is crucified with Christ, the true Self eternally real in God's sustaining love rises from the tomb.

The knowledge of the illuminative way is the intuitive awareness of the divine presence incarnate in the simple *being* of things. It is the graced sensitivity to the inexhaustible depths of holiness inherent in ourselves, in others and in everything around us as flowing immediately from God's creative love. This is the divine inscape that Jesus called us to see in the simplest of things:

"Learn a lesson from the birds," said Jesus. "They do not gather into barns and yet your heavenly Father takes care of them" (cf. Mt. 6:26). The life of a bird is an act of obedience to the Father who gives it life. The actions of the bird are nonactions in that the birds claim nothing for themselves. When they fly, they leave no vapor trail of an "I" to mark the course of their flight. When they fly, they simply fly, free of the dualism of doubt and purpose. Birds form no committees. They offer no ultimatums. When they soar high above the earth, they do so without fear. For even should they fall, their Father knows it, and thus all is well. Since rising high brings no gain, falling brings no loss. In both their rising and their falling, they are simply what they are as held in the arms of the Father whose love they incarnate and express.

"Learn a lesson from the flowers," said Jesus. "Solomon in all his glory was not clothed as one of these" (cf. Mt. 6:29). Flowers are clothed in a glory unpossessed. They radiate a beauty unclaimed. Flowers do not go to the beauty shop. When they pale and begin to wither, nothing is lost for nothing is gained in their coming into bloom. All that they are is what God proclaims them to be in beholding them as eternally present in the Word through whom he sustains them in being. It is the beauty of the Word they incarnate. It is the mystery of the Christ they embody and manifest to us in our intuitive awareness of the Presence they express.

As *A Course in Miracles* so succinctly expresses it:

> Nothing real can be threatened,
> Nothing unreal exists.
> Herein lies the peace of God.*

This is the ontological consciousness of a small child who accepts the kingdom not by its own designs, but by simply being a child. As trusting as a bird on the wing, as fragile as a flower, it reaches out for love, knowing by an innate wisdom that it does so by its birthright as a child of the one who holds it.

We cannot produce this childlike obedience, nor do we have to, for it is inherent in our nature. Our every heartbeat contains the innate wisdom of the birds and flowers. Our every breath expresses the childlike trust in the love that sustains us. We all know something of the childlike wisdom of obeying God by accepting our life as his gift to us. We would go crazy without some degree of this wisdom. We could not carry out our daily tasks if we walked about with our hand on our chest, preoccupied by the nagging concern over how many heartbeats we have left. We could not claim the years have taught us anything if we did not recognize how time and time again the truly formative events of our lives seem to come to us from the depths of a hidden, open-ended pattern beyond our understanding or control.

The problem is, of course, that such insights tend to get lost in the shuffle of daily anxieties and concerns.

*Anonymous. *A Course in Miracles*. Foundation for Inner Peace, 1973, Introduction.

More to the point, the wisdom we all possess by virtue of the obedience inscribed in our nature is, without grace, exiled and lost in a vast disobedience. Having become what we are not through sin, we have become the victims of a cruel ignorance of who we are as children of the Father's love. Instead of using our freedom and consciousness to choose the reality of who we are in God, we have instead gone off into the chimera of egohood and set up shop on our own. As God's grace moves us to repentance, we are restored to the truth of the divine gift given in creation.

Basic to a life of prayer is a childlike reverence for the immediate, concrete realities of everyday living. The wisdom of the contemplative way is to know that taking a walk, tying one's shoe, pouring boiling water into a teacup are incarnations of divine love. The universe is God's body in that it embodies the reality of his love which alone truly is and without which nothing is: You reach out and touch a single drop of water hanging from a leaf—What are you touching really? Who is really touching it?—the first intimations of an answer give birth to a song God sings deep within the heart. Those who hear this song know the bliss that surpasses understanding.

Contemplative prayer is the school in which God instructs his child in the ways of his love. To grow in the wisdom given there is to learn to walk to our place of prayer with a sensitivity to the truth that our every step contains and expresses the union with God we seek. When we sit, we should do so with an unforced reverence for the holiness of sitting. For our sitting is itself our union with God who creates us in our sitting according to an eternal design in Christ the Word. To sit is to obey God. Thus, to sit in a spirit of faith is an incarnation of

Christ. And when we light a candle in a spirit of faith, we celebrate a liturgy of light. Our gazing upon the light is our union with God, who creates us in Christ the eternal light. When we reach out to pick up the scriptures and open them with simple reverence, our action is itself a divine word in which the Father finds his delight and draws us yet closer to himself.

Entrance into the illuminative way necessitates a graced cessation of the projections of the ego self in order to set free a holy silence in which the lesson offered by the birds and flowers is received in our breath, our heartbeat, our simply be-ing who we are:

I sit. The wind blows about the house. A clock ticks. And in my heart there grows a nameless, quiet listening of one who aches for the Father. In this graced stillness I am awakened to my be-ing in Being, which by existential faith I know to be a be-ing in God. This moment of awakening (the eternal ground of all moments) is the moment in which my identity is found in God and God's identity (by his will) is found in me. This is enough. This is everything.

The unitive way is the way of divinization. The knowledge of God given in it is divine knowledge, whereby we know God in an equality of love established by him in the beginning as being our very Self destined to be one with him forever. The divine knowledge of the unitive way transcends and perfects the knowledge of God given in the purgative and illuminative ways.

This is not to suggest that the purgative way is left behind. It continues until the end. Our last breath is a yielding of self that is received into the divine mercy. Until the end we are poured out, filling up what is lacking in the suffering of Christ. Until the end we stumble along, repenting over and over again the same blunder of claiming for ourselves what belongs wholly to God. And in each fall we, by God's grace, meet God catching us in his mercy, restoring us to the truth of who we are in him. Until the end we go to our prayer never really knowing what prayer is, never completely free of the foolishness of striving to possess ourselves even there, in the moment of our self-donation. Until the end the poverty of our prayer is there to lead us to a deeper realization of our total dependency on God's guidance and mercy. It seems that those who give themselves over to prayer are not those who know how to pray, but rather are those who are willing to endure the purifying experience of not knowing how to pray and in this unknowing tasting obscurely yet deeply the divine love that is their life.

Nor does entrance into the unitive way imply that the way of creation is left behind. Christ's resurrection and his promise of our share in it gives testimony to the eternal holiness and reality of our humanity. Our humanity (restored to its original unity with God in Christ through whom it is created) yokes us to God. And in the yoga of simply being human we manifest Christ's presence in the world.

To sit in prayer is our yoga. It is our graced listening to the holiness of our breathing, each breath incarnating the love of the one who gives it. Each breath comes to us as the Christ proclaiming the nearness of God and his love for us. In this listening the veil of ignorance is lifted. The mind of Christ awakens and we come to know (obscurely yet deeply) the divine dimensions of all that is human:

An old woman washes out a bowl. A married couple looks down into the face of their sleeping infant, their hearts impaled by its haunting beauty. A man runs along a city street. And you sit silent and still, your breathing

marking the cadences of the unseen giftedness that sus-
tains us all. Sitting thus, we give witness to the truth:
There is no end to the holiness of our lives, for our
humanity is grounded in the eternal God for whom we
were created and in whom we live as his body.

But while the knowledge of God given in the
purgative and illuminative ways is not left behind, neither
is it the highest form of contemplative knowledge of God
that is possible on this earth. The mystics assure us of the
reality of a unitive knowledge of God in which (in the
obscurity of naked faith) one knows God as God knows
God, and loves God as God loves God. They assure us of
the possibility of being awakened to one's unity with God
before he said, "let it be."

In searching for a metaphor that might provide some
degree of insight into this fullness of contemplative
wisdom characteristic of the unitive way, we turn now to
the notion of the Self as presented in the thought of Dan
Walsh.* Walsh's reflections begin in the beginning. He
asks, What is absolutely first in God's creation of us in
his image and likeness? What has absolute primacy over
everything else in the first love of God's personal creation? And in response to this inquiry Walsh answers that
what God first creates is a simple capacity for divine love.

"Before creation . . . God had not the capacity to
love himself. There was no capacity for love in God."
Capacity implies potentiality, lack, the ability to reach
some as yet unrealized goal. An empty cup, for example,
has the capacity for water, whereas a cup already filled to
overflowing has none. It is full. Similarly, "before creation," God, the eternal, superabundant fullness of Love

*The reader is asked to recall what was written in the Preface concern-
ing Walsh and his philosophy of the person. All quotes in this section
are taken from a conference by Walsh.

itself has no capacity for love. God as God has no lack of divine love, for he is this Love itself. The mystery of God's personal creation is that he creates this lack of his own fullness.

God, in the pure and gratuitous freedom of love, creates the capacity to receive the love he is. And this capacity is who we are! It is our true self as a relation of likeness without difference to God in his love. It is our ultimate identity as a *capax dei,* a simple capacity for God.

There is then in the beginning no self. There is no separate self *with* a relation to God, but rather self that *is* a relation to God. There is in the beginning no dualistic other, no ego, no separateness, but rather a simple God-us unity in divine love, a simple capacity to receive all that God is. And we are this unity, this relation, this capacity.

Now, how is this capacity for God to reach fulfillment? How is the divine union that is our innermost self to be realized? To this Walsh answers that personal union with God is realized through our nature. Our human nature is our means to personal fulfillment. Without nature there would only be God in God's personal creation—God as God and God as the capacity to receive all that God is. Thus, God makes this capacity "real." He "endows it with being. . . . He gives it a nature." Our created human nature comes in to fulfill the created capacity for love. It is through our nature as created human beings that we are empowered to consent freely to God's will for us to be one with him by the fact that his love at the core of our being elicits this consent. It is through our humanity that we freely reciprocate divine love and thereby bring to fulfillment who we are in that love.

From the vantage point of this anthropology of divine love we can arrive at some degree of insight into the unitive way of contemplative union with God: There is the contemplative prayer of the purgative way in which we know God in and through our fallen human nature in its encounter with the cross—a great undoing in mercy—a journey through apparent loss and meaninglessness in which a gift is given. There is the contemplative prayer of the illuminative way in which God is known in the awareness of our human nature restored through our share in the cross to its original transparency to divine love. There is the quiet, joyful intuitive awareness that our sitting, our standing, our simply being who we are is God's incarnate ecstasy in the immediacy of the present moment before thought begins.

And there is the contemplative prayer of the unitive way in which our humanity is fulfilled in being utterly transcended in the awakening of the Self that is God's kingdom. There is the realization of the divine gift given in the first love of God's personal creation—the gift of God enraptured and lost in us as awakened to and lost in him. There is the manifestation of the God-us unity in which we are forever rooted in the nuptials of God's ecstatic love.

Walsh presents us with an anthropology of love in which love precedes and perfects nature. Unity precedes and perfects diversity. Who we are in God's ecstatic love precedes and perfects what we become in the world. For Walsh,

"God first creates not a thing," not a created human nature, but first he creates a person, a simple capacity to receive his love. And then in that relationship (called person) God creates a nature. He endows that relation with reality in being. "Once God creates the capacity for love, then he concreates (with it . . . con) the nature. He concreates man, angel. In that you have what has come to be the historical you and the historical me, the moral you and the moral me, the physical you and the physical me. Before that there is the spiritual you."

It is this spiritual identity that awakens in the divine knowledge of the unitive way. Beyond knowing and not knowing, beyond being and not being, beyond sin and no sin, yet within, utterly within, God's love (being the ALL which alone truly is in and of itself) finds in us a corresponding point of absolute nothingness. God discovers in us an inexhaustible emptiness in which he perfectly pours himself out in the self-ecstasy of his creative love. And our nothingness, being boundless, offers no resistance, no confinement to his outpouring.

In reflecting on this primal unity with God that is our identity in him, Meister Eckhart writes,

> In this likeness or identity God takes such delight that he pours his whole nature and being into it. His pleasure is as great, to take a simile, as that of a horse, let loose over a green heath, where the ground is level and smooth, to gallop as a horse will, as fast as he can over the greensward—for this is a horse's pleasure and nature. It is so with God. It is his pleasure and rapture to discover identity, because he can always put his whole being into it—for he is this identity itself (Blackney, *Meister Eckhart,* p. 205).

How are we to enter into the unitive way? How is it that our humanity weakened by sin yet restored to God through Christ becomes our means to divine union? This, in effect, is the disciples' question: How can I discover that living awareness of the God-us unity that is life itself? In the contemplative-mystical traditions of spiritual direction, this is the one root question that brings master and disciple together.

In the sayings of the Desert Fathers we find this story which provides an insight into how the unitive way is to be found:

> Abbot Lot came to Abbot Joseph and said: Father, according as I am able, I keep my little rule, and my little fast, my prayer, meditation and contemplative silence; and according as I am able I strive to cleanse my heart of thoughts: now what more should I do? The elder rose up in reply and stretched out his hands to heaven, and his fingers became like ten lamps of fire. He said: Why not be totally changed into fire? (Thomas Merton, *Wisdom of the Desert,* New Directions 1960, p. 50).

The response of Abbot Joseph turned Abbot Lot's question to ashes. If he received the message he, no doubt, returned to his cell a changed man, for he would no longer seek God according as *he* was able. He would continue to pray, to fast, to keep his rule but from a wholly new point of view; namely, that of a deep faith in what God is able to achieve in him by his all-gracious and powerful will.

Detached from any naive assumptions about the importance of anything he might say or not say, do or not do, feel or not feel, Abbot Lot turns to God. In facing his helplessness and ignorance regarding how to begin the search for God, he lets God be God. And upon the lowered face of Abbot Lot there begins to shine the divine light of the unitive way.

Huang Po, the ninth-century Zen master, stated, in effect, that as long as we are still striving for a goal, we have not yet begun. What alone truly matters begins in nameless silence and with "the suddenness of a knife thrust," a great death to the ignorance that has for so long held us captive:

You are walking alone just before sunset in an old and deserted cemetery. The birds sing. The tall grass partially hides the row upon row of stones, each marking the earthly remains of a life as hidden, as unique as your own. "How am I to enter into deeper intimacy with God?" you ask as a way of expressing a prayer that has long since become your life's desire. And then you become aware that perhaps the question itself presupposes and nurtures the ignorance that hides this union from your awareness.

You sit beneath a tree. Just sitting. Nothing happens. No feeling. No thought. No absence of thought or feeling. . . . The stream of thought is broken. The self that asks is no more. Yet, nothing is broken. All is as it was before. Out of one's repentant silence, out of one's blundering ways, out of a graced and love-filled waiting, out of nowhere, out of God . . . the gift of God is given. . . . Realization! Awakening! God is ALL and all that is is God's. No. This is not enough—the unity I am in him and who he is in me manifests itself, leaving no trace of a self apart to receive the gift, no God apart to give it. Self beyond self! God beyond God!

Yet this is not what it is like at all, not at all. Nothing that can be spoken is. Nothing that can be thought approaches it. Thus, without knowing anything, with nothing to say, filled with gratitude and humbled by God's goodness you stand and walk on in the darkness. You note once again the stones, standing milky white in the moonlight, marking the company you keep—a great cloud of witnesses, those who walked with God but are seen no more because God took them (Heb 11:5).

St. John of the Cross devoted all of the second book of *The Ascent of Mount Carmel* to the theme of faith, through which, in this life, we know God. He begins by citing the second stanza of the poem on which *The Ascent* and *The Dark Night* depend for their original inspiration and pivotal metaphors. The stanza reads:

> In darkness and secure
> By the secret ladder, disguised,
> Ah the sheer grace!—
> In darkness and concealment
> My house being now all stilled;

His reflections begin with the poetic image of "the secret ladder disguised":

> The "secret ladder" represents faith, because all the rungs or articles of faith are secret to and hidden from both the senses and the intellect. Accordingly the soul lived in darkness, without the light of the senses and intellect, and went out beyond every natural and rational boundary to climb the divine ladder of faith that leads up to and penetrates the deep things of God (1 Cor 2:1). (*The Ascent,* Bk. II, chap. 1, no. 1).

Imagine yourself walking alone at night searching for God. You cross a vast, windswept field, and there in the center of the field you come upon a ladder that ascends up through the darkness into the depths of the living God. The ladder is faith, and its rungs are the articles of faith. The rungs are solid and secure and can be trusted in your ascent toward God:

> . . . The likeness between faith and God is so close that no other difference exists than that between believing in God and seeing him. Just as God is infinite, faith proposes Him as infinite; as there are Three Persons in One God, it presents Him to us in this way . . . (*The Ascent,* Bk. II, chap. 9, no. 1).

In beginning your ascent the truth of faith informs you that each article of faith is an invitation to ascend higher into the depths of transforming intimacy with God. God eternally draws us into union with himself, and this is the way faith presents him to us. In an obscure manner that is itself a mystery of faith God touches the inner heart revealing himself to be the one who touches hearts. He awakens us to his love, thereby manifesting himself to us as the awakener, the one who delivers us from being oblivious to his presence. This personal encounter with God in faith reveals to us that each article of faith is a transparent metaphor of divine love, a specific facet of the one who calls us into union with himself.

The intimacy with God that faith reveals unfolds in a luminous darkness. Faith is luminous in that it enlightens. By its light we see the Light. But faith is dark as well in that the divine light remains hidden even as it is seen. Faith is dark in that in its wisdom we remain unable to understand. In its giftedness we possess nothing. In the journey on which it calls us we go nowhere, except into a heightened awareness of and sensitivity to the presence of God in the present moment. Thus, the ascent of faith is an interior movement of transformation in which,

> The soul declares it was disguised, because in the ascent through faith its garments, apparel, and capacities were changed from natural to divine. Because of this disguise, neither the devil, nor temporal, nor rational things recognized or detained it. None of these can do harm to the man who walks in faith (*The Ascent,* Bk. II, chap. 1, no. 1).

How does this transformation from the natural to the divine take place? It takes place through our entering into each truth of faith, as into a holy place prepared for us by God so that we might surrender to his saving presence and thus come to know him in the intimacy of that surrender. We say "Our Father . . ." and yield in the words to our Father's presence. We proclaim our faith in being Christ's body, the church, and yield to the truth of the unity with God in Christ we profess.

It is in the subtle secrecy of faith's sweet surrender that God is obscurely known precisely as God, who calls us beyond the limitations of our thoughts and feelings into the intimacy of his loving presence. No rational explanation can account for or bring about this radical centering in eternal love. Thus, when given over to God in simple, childlike faith we are hidden from everything rational. In this freedom and detachment from the ability to understand or explain, nothing rational can detain us.

Likewise, nothing temporal can account for or bring about this obscure intimacy in which the disciple cries, "Abba." The gift of knowing God in faith is not limited to time, nor is it received in such a way as to be subject to time's vacillations. It is eternal knowledge given by God to those who open themselves to his eternal love. Thus, when given over to God in simple, childlike faith we are hidden from everything temporal. In this freedom and detachment from all that begins and ends in time nothing temporal can detain us.

And when grounded in a faith surrender to the living God we are as well hidden from the devil, for he cannot see the one who belongs to God in faith: The devil enters a room filled with people hidden in faith. For him the room is empty. One person begins to doubt and a face appears in the emptiness. The devil sees only what is unreal in us, what in us shares in his enigmatic, self-chosen illusion of separation from God. If the devil could see who we really are (and who he really is!) in God, he would see

God. The mystery of evil he personified is his blindness to our reality as persons created in the image and likeness of God. Thus, surrendered to God in faith, we are hidden from the devil. Nothing evil can detain us.

What is it that empowers faith to bring us into the awareness of the living God? The answer cannot lie in anything created. As St. John of the Cross reminds us,

> . . . all means must be proportionate to their end. That is, they must manifest a certain accord with and likeness to the end—of such a degree that they would be sufficient for the attainment of the desired goal.
>
> For example, if a man wants to reach a city, he must necessarily take the road, the means that leads to the city (*The Ascent,* Bk. II, chap. 8, no. 2).

There is, however, no proportion of likeness or accord between the finite and the infinite, between the creature and God. The saint writes,

> Though truly, as theologians say, all creatures carry with them a certain relationship to God and a trace of Him (greater or less according to his perfection of their being), yet God has no relation or essential likeness to them. Rather the difference which lies between His divine being and their being is infinite. Consequently, intellectual comprehension of God through heavenly or earthly creatures is impossible, since there is no proportion of likeness. . . . Thus no creature can serve the intellect as a proportionate means to the attainment of God. . . . Nothing that could possibly be imagined or comprehended in this life can be a proximate means to union with God (*The Ascent,* Bk. II, chap. 8, nos. 3-4).

We who are finite seek union with the infinite actuality of God. Our dilemma is that our finite intellects and the finite means at our disposal, such as all we can think, imagine or comprehend of God in this life, are disproportioned to God. Faith is God's response to this dilemma. God's gift of faith nullifies the disproportion between himself and the mind of the one to whom he reveals himself. In faith God penetrates the mind with a proportional likeness to himself, a participatory sharing in the divine light in which he knows himself. Thus, faith is also darkness to us insofar as our knowledge in this life remains dependent upon the finite powers of the senses, memory, imagination and conceptualizing mind. For these finite modalities of knowing are transcended in the divine mode of knowing that interpenetrates and transforms the mind in faith.

There is, of course, a finite, conceptual context in which faith is received. Indeed, "faith comes through hearing" (Rom 10:17). But in order to know God through what is heard it is necessary to stay free, open and unencumbered by the finite context of the words so as to resonate with the infinite. For in calling us to faith God calls us to release our hold upon the finite, so that he can lead us into a deep, living knowledge of him uniting us to himself in Christ the Word. Faith, then, is the royal road that leads to the end, which is God. This is so because faith is not of this world, but of God. Therefore, it does God's work of dislodging us from our dependence on the finite by drawing us out beyond our creatureliness into God.

It is in this vein that the saint quotes the book of Isaiah, "If you do not believe you will not understand" (Is 7:9). That is, unless you surrender to God your ability to understand, you will never understand. But if you make this surrender of childlike faith, you will in the very surrender of your understanding begin to understand.

For faith brings us into the living awareness of a union with God. This is simply beyond, indeed infinitely beyond, the reach of our finite modes of understanding. So it is that,

> A man . . . is decidedly hindered from the attainment of this high state of union with God when he is attached to any understanding, feeling, imagining, opinion, desire or way of his own, or to any other of his works or affairs, and knows not how to detach and denude himself of these impediments. His goal transcends all of this, even the loftiest object that can be known or experienced. Consequently, he must pass beyond everything into unknowing (*The Ascent,* Bk. II, chap. 4, no. 4).

To foster this movement toward unknowing in naked faith, the saint quotes Hebrews 11:6 which reads, "He who would approach union with God should believe in his existence." He then states,

> This is like saying: to attain union with God, a person should advance neither by understanding, nor by the support of his own experience, nor by feeling or imagination, but by belief in God's presence.* For God's presence cannot be grasped by the intellect, appetite, imagination or any other sense, nor can it be known in this life (*The Ascent,* Bk. II, chap. 4, no. 4).

It is in our prayer that this passing beyond everything into unknowing, this turning of one's whole self toward the divine presence is most singularly expressed. In a manner that is itself hidden and unknown to the one who experiences it, the transformation begins. Through one's

---

*I have chosen to use the term "presence," instead of the term "being."

fidelity to silent, heartfelt prayer, one discovers that words, thoughts and feelings become less and less capable of capturing the unseen, essentially unfelt fire that burns within.

As one sits in contemplative stillness one witnesses—without seeing anything—the unprecedented undoing of the heart. Without going anywhere one is taken up secretly into the abyss of presence that is God. Without perceptible incident one is unclothed of one's own abilities and modes of understanding. In ways unknown, one ceases to see in the light of one's own understanding and begins instead to see in the light of God, which remains dark and hidden to external ego consciousness. It is as though the poverty and silence of prayer has become a barren wilderness in which one suddenly discovers the road that leads to union:

> As regards this road to union, entering on the road means leaving one's own road, or better, moving on to the goal; and turning from one's own mode implies entry into what has no mode, that is, God. A person who reaches this state no longer has any modes or methods, still less is he—nor can he be—attached to them. I am referring to modes of understanding, taste, and feeling. Within himself, though, he possesses all methods, like one who though having nothing yet possesses all things (2 Cor 6:10). By being courageous enough to pass beyond the interior and exterior limits of his nature, he enters within supernatural bounds—bounds that have no mode, yet in substance possess all modes. To reach the supernatural bounds a person must depart from his natural bounds and leave self far off in respect to his interior and exterior limits in order to mount from a low state to the highest (*The Ascent,* Bk. II, chap. 4, no. 5).

A mode refers to a specific way of being that defines us and gives shape and substance to our lives. Sex, age, religion, political persuasion, health, geographical location—all are modalities of being which taken collectively constitute what we customarily think of as our "self."

God, however, has no mode. He is not restricted to any way of being. He is not here to the exclusion of there. He is neither male nor female. He never began, nor will he ever cease to be, thus he is at once ever ancient and ever new. He is not within to the exclusion of being all around and beyond. He is not transcendent to the exclusion of being intimately known to those whom he calls to share his life. He is not intimately known to the exclusion of remaining transcendent, beyond all that is known. No category contains him. He has no mode, and yet he possesses all modes as their author, as the ALL that sustains them in being.

By being courageous enough to leave self far off with respect to all exterior and interior limits of one's own being, one leaves behind all modalities of being, one shares in the infinite richness which is at once the infinite poverty of God. Through faith incarnate in contemplative wisdom the "general loving awareness" proper to contemplation gives birth to a new life hidden in God.

Of course, in terms of nature one is still as limited, as mode-bound as before. In terms of external, objective consciousness nothing happens. One is still here to the exclusion of there. One is still a certain age, one still lives in a certain set of patterns, and so on. But the point is *none* of these modalities touches what has become the hidden ALL, the unseen center of one's life lost in God. For to the extent one is transformed in faith, one's life becomes less and less "one's life" (for the "one" who claims this set of modalities as its own does not appear in the contemplative silence where a new life in God is found in being lost in God forever). The modalities continue. One is still male or female, healthy or sick, and all the rest, but they are there as unpossessed and as incapable of possessing us, of defining us, for who we *really* are is possessed by Love alone. And yet in this freedom, this perfect dispossession, this nonattachment, all modes are possessed, not as possessions (for there is no "owner" to claim them), but as capacities for gratitude, awe, compassion, and all that makes our lives real in God's presence:

I sit in prayer. My sitting is a mode of being. But when surrendered over to God in prayer my sitting in no way determines the reality of the moment. As hidden in faith, I sit beyond sitting. I am silent in prayer, but my silence in no way determines the true dimensions of the unnamed Silence that utters me forever in love. I am poor in prayer, knowing nothing. But my poverty in no way determines the true poverty of the cross that now unfolds within me, dispersing the "me" I think myself to be, until God alone is left living in me lost in him. I am afraid of this undoing, this crucifixion of all that is less than God. This is why I live in the diaspora of my compromises, why even now I experience my evasions from the union with God I seek.

But here is where God's mercy is manifested in the poverty of silent prayer. For by allowing Christ's indwelling Spirit to lead me to this unseen axis of truth, in mounting this place of my deliverance, in being firmly nailed in place in the dispersion of all I cling to as constituting my life—I discover the unexpected joy of God. In this espousal to Love crucified I am carried, through the obscurity of faith, into an ineffable communion.

I am just myself. I get up every morning. I go to bed every night. And yet, "It is not I who live, but Christ who lives in me" (Gal 2:20). One can hardly speak of it, for there is nothing to talk about except that a great undoing in love keeps breaking the connections. Every time one seems to get close to understanding, to being secure, to having arrived, it all comes apart in a painful inadequacy, a sense of self-betrayal. The voice within (which is not heard) speaks: "You are mine. There is for you no closure, no arriving, no rest except in me. When you waver in weakness I will meet you in mercy. When you are lost I will be the land unknown in which you wander. Live this way and although you will know nothing, my wisdom will be yours. Although you will possess nothing I myself am yours, for you are forever mine. To you in your blindness this way of living is radical, a death you cannot comprehend. It is nonetheless simply living in the truth of who you are in me. It is simply being who I create you to be. There is, really, no other way, for nothing else is real save in me."

This way is the way of no mode; no this or that, no plans, no list of gains and losses, no self to make the lists, to formulate the next plan. It is the way infinitely given in every breath and heartbeat. It is the ALL that really is. For this is what it means to fulfill God's will, by loving God in such a way that one labors,

> . . . to divest and deprive oneself for God of all that is not God. When this is done the soul will be illumined by and transformed in God. And God will so communicate His supernatural being to it that it will appear to be God Himself and will possess all that God Himself has (*The Ascent,* Bk. II, chap. 5, no. 7).

Faith, then, for St. John of the Cross amounts to nothing less than a transformation in God, who is the un-created fullness for whom we are created and without whom we are nothing. He searches for metaphors that might give some hint as to what this transforming union in faith is like:

He says it is like a log in a fire. At first the log is com-pletely different than the fire. As it begins to receive the fire's heat it sputters and cracks, as if to complain of the undoing the fire is causing. This undoing, however, results in a transformation in which, "the log becomes all fiery and one cannot distinguish the log from the fire" (Cf. *The Living Flame of Love,* Stanza 1, art. 2-6).

He says that the transformation can be likened to sit-ting very, very still as the Beloved etches his perfect likeness upon the heart. Every movement, that is, every attachment, every turning in desire for some creature, every clinging to an idea, only makes the etching more difficult to achieve (*The Dark Night,* Bk. I, chap. 10, no. 5).

He says in effect that when we are transformed in faith our mother is a virgin, for the self-in-faith is not born of the will of the flesh, but of the will of God. It is the Spirit's work, bringing to birth the self hidden with Christ in God (*The Ascent,* Bk. II, chap. 5, no. 5).

He says the soul transformed in the union with God realized in faith can be likened to a window through which the sun is shining. All of one's attachments are like smudges that make the window visible.

> . . . If (however) the window is totally clean and pure, the sunlight will so transform and illumine it that to all appearances the window will be identical with the ray of sunlight and shine just as the sun's ray (*The Ascent,* Bk. II, chap. 5, no. 6).

He then continues,

> When God grants this supernatural favor to the
> soul, so great a union is caused that all the things of
> both God and the soul become one in participant
> transformation, and the soul appears to be God
> more than a soul. Indeed, it is God by participation.
> Yet truly, its being (even though transformed) is
> naturally as distinct from God's as it was before,
> just as the window, although illumined by the ray,
> has an existence distinct from the ray (*The Ascent*,
> Bk. II, chap. 5, no. 7).

How are we to understand these and similar passages
regarding the mystical union between God and the one
who seeks him? Not literally, that is, St. John of the
Cross is not stating that in this transforming union the
created human being ceases to be a created human and
becomes instead God. That is, the union is not a substantial union. Just as the window in the sun's ray does not
become the sun, neither does the soul in this union cease
being the soul in becoming perfectly one with God.

But neither are these and similar passages to be taken
figuratively, as though they are nothing more than poetic
imagery. Nothing could be further from the truth. The
imagery of perfect union with God used by St. John of
the Cross, the author of *The Cloud of Unknowing,* and
the other mystics, refer to a divine transformation of the
very foundations of one's being. For the one who experiences this transformation, though hidden in the
obscurity of faith, it is the most real of all realities, the
touchstone with Reality itself.

How are we to understand the passages in St. John
of the Cross and the other mystics about mystical union
with God? By reading the passages *as an act of faith*. And

this means to read them from the vantage point of the desire for this union that God has placed within us. In this way, by God's grace, we can in our reading pass through the words into unknowing, in which God is known in a secret consummation of love.

6 THE PURIFICATION OF THE SENSES

To know God in the obscure depths of contemplative love is to know as well the need to purify the mind of the tendency to cling to, and thereby limit one's self to any idea of God. The contemplative way is that of naked faith, through which one is led in poverty and great longing beyond all concepts and images into a deep hidden knowledge of our union with God in Christ.

This same self-emptying, self-transcending process is necessary with respect to bodily desires and the entire range of sensory experience. The beginner in the contemplative way faces the task of cooperating with God in undergoing a metamorphosis of daily consciousness in which one is set free from the tendency to feed the egocentric self with a continual flow of sensory experiences to which one clings with a possessive heart.

Such an assertion raises some practical questions: In striving to free myself from sensory attachments, how do I avoid an unhealthy, unnatural refusal to enjoy the goodness of the body and all of God's creation? Does the necessity of purifying the senses mean I am to approach a piece of ripe fruit, a glass of sherry, or a Mozart concerto with reservations or even a tinge of guilt? How am I to separate the chaff from the wheat, that is, how am I to preserve what is wholesome and genuine in sensory experience while at the same time freeing myself from those elements of sensory experience that block the full realization of union with God in prayer?

In response to such questions, it is first necessary to affirm the goodness and holiness of bodily desires and all that comes to us through the senses. Sensory experiences and bodily desires are not alien forces from which we are to try to exorcise ourselves. The opposite is true: Our senses and the urge to gratify ourselves through them are manifestations of our being. The at-times restless urgency of sensual impulses is an expression of our solidarity with the ebb and flow of life that courses through the whole of nature. And ultimately the dynamism of the senses expresses our ontological-spiritual solidarity with God. Ultimately our senses express our capacity to receive the One who creates our senses and bodily desires and who is alone their sole ultimate fulfillment.

Thus, to be at odds with sensory pleasure and experience is to be at odds with ourselves, with reality and, ultimately, at odds with God, who creates our bodily existence and who in Christ has claimed it as his own.

Here, then, is a guiding principle of the purification of the senses required to reach union with God: Return to the senses, return to a healthy, normal acceptance of bodily existence in God's presence. One of the most common forms of abuse of this basic principle is that of the tendency to affirm one's ego self in a driving push toward some goal. In its most blatant expressions this form of alienation results in neglecting one's bodily and emotional health as well as one's personal relationships in order to reach some treasured goal. This can happen in a religious context, as illustrated by the following story found in Martin Buber's *Hasidism and Modern Man* (Harper Torch Books, 1958, pp. 31-32):

> In order that his study in the holy books should not suffer too long interruption, Rabbi Shmelke used to sleep in no other way than sitting, his head on his arm; but between his fingers he held a burning candle that awakened him as soon as the flame touched his hand. When Rabbi Eimelech visited him and recognized the still imprisoned might of his holiness, he carefully prepared for him a couch and induced him with much persuasion to stretch himself out on it for a while. Then he shut and darkened the window. Rabbi Shmelke only awoke when it was already broad daylight. He noticed how long he had slept, but it did not bother him; for he felt an unknown, sunlike clarity. He went into the prayer house and prayed before the community as was his custom. To the community, however, it appeared as if they had never before heard him, so did the might of his holiness compel and liberate all. When he sang the song of the Red Sea, they had to pull up their caftans in order that the waves rearing up to the right and the left should not wet them.

Rabbi Schmelke is no stranger. We can recognize him in ourselves, in our unholy zeal with which we abuse our need for sleep, a balanced diet or a relaxing meal with a friend. As subject to this self-abuse we find ourselves to be spiritually emasculated, too tired, too fragmented to pray.

Sometimes the situation is such that we are left with no choice but to push ourselves to the point of exhaustion. Sometimes our exhaustion is the only prayer we can offer, for it is all we have. This is the prayer of the poor, of those who labor simply to survive, and it is a prayer to which God is always attentive. Rabbi Shmelke, however, suffered from an unholy exhaustion remedied only by obeying the limits that God has established in the gift of our bodies. The imprisoned might of our holiness is set free in our humble reverence for the God-given necessities of bodily existence. When accepted in a spirit of faith, our bodily needs prove not to be limits at all, but instead the sanctuary where God unexpectedly manifests the truth that our bodily existence embodies his presence.

This truth is foundational. It is the incarnational principle of the contemplative way. In the practice of contemplative prayer it is not enough merely to sit while we pray. What is needed is to follow our sitting like we would a friend into the simplicity and nondualistic miracle of "just sitting." To just sit is our way. It is sitting thus, free of the complexities of means and ends, that the imprisoned might of our holiness is set free. This might is that of God's creative love which our sitting incarnates.

Similarly, in the practice of contemplative prayer, we do not listen to our breathing in the dualistic sense in which our breathing is an object of our speculation. Rather, our contemplative awareness of our breath is such that we are led, as by a faithful friend, into the loving presence of God breathing into us the gift of his life. "Just breathing" is our way. For in our humble letting go of every idea, every goal, we are set free to discover *now,* in *this* breath the eternal immediacy of God.

The same holds true of our beating heart. Each beat is the bench mark of God's nearness. If our heart stops today, tomorrow's plans are cancelled. If we sit in prayer and our heart stops, our search for God meets with sudden, unplanned success. Such is God's nearness. Such is the thread that flows from God and with which we weave the fabric of our lives. Thus, to sit in contemplative stillness is to follow each heartbeat as one would a faithful friend into God's humble sovereignty, his life-giving nearness. God waits to be discovered in the red, wet wonder of our blood. Our way to God is that of our following his awakening call into his presence incarnate in our beating heart.

The purification of the senses with respect to the search for intimacy with God in prayer refers, then, to our letting go of the obsessions that alienate us from the reality and holiness of our bodily being. The process is that of a humble return to the Father's house, which is one's unique bodily being that embodies the gift of God's presence.

This return to the Father's house consists of a process of conversion from goal-dominated consciousness to a detached, open awareness of the divine dimensions of the present moment. The tendency to affirm the ego-self in a driving push toward goals is but a symptom of a goal-dominated modality of consciousness in which the reason why one is doing something tends to overpower the awareness of simply doing what one is doing. This modality of goal consciousness tends to be pervasive, becoming one's mode of being in the world.

To live in this way is rarely to allow oneself to become aware of being oneself in the present moment because one is dominated by some goal to be realized in some future moment. The present moment tends, then, to be a means toward getting somewhere else which when reached becomes the means of yet more goals. Thus, one tends never to read a book but to read it with the goal of finishing it so as to begin another book. One tends never to take a walk, but to walk with the goal of getting someplace, which then becomes the means of getting someplace else.

To live in this way is to be subject to judgment, for one is always evaluating the present moment by the criterion of how quickly, how efficiently, or how cleverly one's goals are being reached. More precisely, one is always evaluating oneself in the scale of some goal.

As the story of Rabbi Shmelke illustrates, the religious realm is not exempt from dualistic goal consciousness. In fact, prayer itself tends to get pulled into this mode of being in the world. Union with God in prayer becomes a goal and one's imagined progress in prayer is determined by how well one perceives this goal is being achieved. Very often both spiritual pride and discouragement in prayer can be attributed to this dualistic, judgmental mentality of weighing prayer on the scales of a goal.

True prayer rises spontaneously in goal-less-ness. If when we sit in prayer we sit with no goal, then there is no place for either discouragement or spiritual pride to take hold. The very notions of progress or the lack of progress cease to have meaning when one is no longer going anywhere. When we "just sit" we enter into the way of goal-less-ness, the nondualistic way of simply being who we are in the reality of the present moment.

This may sound irresponsible, but actually the opposite is true. For our preoccupation with goals is, in effect, our irresponsibility to the supreme task of being present to God in the present moment. It is our goal of prayer and not our failure to reach it that is our true obstacle to entering into the contemplative way. For our imagined goal is the expression of our ignorance of the consummate union with God that is even now the hidden ground of the present moment.

Of course, at one level goals in prayer are both inevitable and helpful. When held lightly as that which directs us toward self-giving love, a goal is itself a gift of love. But when clung to as a self-devised end in itself, a goal is an idol, a projected image of one's own idealized self and is thus an obstacle to divine union.

It is by our patient endurance of the poverty of our prayer that we allow God to topple the idols that stand in the way of divine union. When we sit in prayer freed by God of all imaginary goals we face the possibility of realizing the truth of our sitting as rising immediately from the ground of divine love that eternally creates it and which it therefore eternally expresses. When we sit in goal-less-ness and turn to glance at a shadow cast upon the floor, we are on the brink of a free fall into the divine awakening of the truth of our glance as rising immediately from its eternal ground, as does the shadow, as does all that is.

The wisdom of prayer is expressed in a paradox. If we find ourselves falling asleep during prayer we should take steps to stay awake. But we should do so without letting staying awake become a goal. We should do so with a reverence for the divine dimensions of sleepiness. If we find ourselves being distracted during prayer, we should take steps not to be distracted. But we should do so without letting freedom of distractions become a goal. We should do so with a reverence for the divine dimensions of the mind, which in its intricate complexity and ceaseless activity manifests something of the infinite possibilities and eternal activity of God.

The giftedness of prayer—a giftedness we can hardly bear—is the giftedness of God's transcendent imminence, his radical nearness in which no matter where we turn, he is there as the eternal ground of all that is. More than this—he is the eternal ground of our deepest Self. Before we turn anywhere he is the abyss beneath our feet, a love unknown hidden in the palms of our hands, the warmth of our breath, our most fleeting, most secret thought, our simply being who we are. There is nowhere to escape, for the escape itself would be an escape in him in whom all that is is one. For God is God, uniting us to himself in the unity of his love prior to anything that is this or that, prior to any goal attained or not attained.

Goal-less-ness is not difficult. It is impossible. If it were possible, it would be a goal, something one might possibly attain. Instead, goal-less-ness is death to the goal-seeking self that is the birth that begins in God's awakening call to union with himself. The call is followed in the patient endurance of one's poverty in prayer. It is followed in learning to be content with the unseen richness of having nothing. It is followed in surrendering to the Presence unknown, in uttering Abba silently within the heart, in following the Spirit's promptings leading us into a union with God that fulfills his will for us to be one with him in the simplicity of childlike faith.

The interior transformation resulting from our journey back to the Father's house (consisting of the truth of our bodily being in the present moment) brings one into the center of a great mystery: The divine perfection calls us to itself, causing our every imperfection to signal the need to move on, to continue the struggle to conform ourselves to God's will for us to be perfect, even as our heavenly Father is perfect (Mt 5:48). And yet somehow each imperfection mysteriously incarnates the divine presence as the place where God waits to meet us, like a father prodigal with love, embracing us with mercy, within mercy. Similarly, the eternal presence of God stirs within us, causing a discontent with all that is subject to time. And yet somehow each moment is forever, never to be lost in him for whom a thousand years are as a day (2 Pt 3:8) and each moment, this moment, is as eternal as the ground from which it eternally springs.

Here, where God's unconditional love, our true Self hidden in him and the depths of the netherworld meet, there is mystery and paradox. But even more there is the quiet assurance that this is the moment to pass secretly through all that one understands and does not understand into the divine embrace. For this is the moment of Presence, the moment of Love alone.

Inordinate sensual gratification is another expression of our alienation from our bodily wholeness in God's presence. Here the flight from the divine dimensions of the present moment is not expressed as, "I am the goals I attain," but rather as "I am the pleasures I enjoy, the pains I must suffer." It is in experiencing our vulnerability to this tendency to restrict one's horizons to what is available to the senses that one learns to appreciate the value of fasting and other ascetical practices. Of course, if carried out as a goal to affirm one's image of oneself as someone who fasts, then fasting is but one more tangential maneuver on the way to God. If carried out with some kind of antagonism toward the body, then fasting is but a way of feeding an illusion with an illusion. But if carried out with prudence and relaxed seriousness as an expression of the desire for deeper intimacy with God, then fasting can occasion the realization of that desire.

Devotional fasting is never private, for it expresses one's solidarity with all of humanity in our shared hunger for food and ultimately for God. At the same time devo-

tional fasting is always personal. How one fasts is unique
to each person, but the following paradigm is offered to
suggest a tone or spirit that is conducive to a contemplative awareness of the mystery that fasting expresses.

The night before your day of fast, you pray that your
fasting will foster a deepened hunger and thirst for God.
Then upon rising the next morning you renew this sense
of expressing your hunger and thirst for God through
your day of fasting, praying that God will lead you
beyond the senses into a deeper, living awareness of your
union with him in Christ the Word. To incarnate this
desire for deeper intimacy with God, you abstain from all
food and water until sunset. As the day proceeds you
meet each moment of hunger or thirst as though meeting
a friend, telling you of God and the need to seek him
above all else.

Then in the evening you sit alone in silent prayer
before a piece of bread and a glass of wine or a glass of
water. As a verbal expression of the grace of the day you
repeat over and over the words of the psalmist, "As a
heart longs for flowing streams, so my soul for thee, O
God" (Ps 42:1). You listen to your thirst as to a wise
friend sent by God in the beginning to draw you into the
eternal waters of divine love. You listen to your hunger,
following it through faith into a holy communion with
God. In this way you meet the living God waiting for you
to eat and drink. In obedience to his will you eat in
gratitude, tasting in the bread the incarnate nearness of
the One you seek and now meet in the act of eating. In
obedience to his will you drink in this ritual celebrating
your union with God.

Perhaps this evening agape, this eucharistic communion, could be entered into by participation in an evening liturgy or perhaps with a supper with loved ones. Perhaps one's health or situation or inclination does not permit such a day of fast. No matter. What is important is that we use what is available to us to enter through the senses into a deeper, more intimate awareness of our union with God.

Our prayer is our fasting. When we sit in contemplative stillness we abstain from all that is less than love. We let go of our dependency on the goals that alienate us from the eternal now of God's love. We loosen our hold on thoughts and feelings. We pass unseen by every mortal eye through the vast emptiness between consolation and aridity. We die to the self limited to and imprisoned within the confines of this or that, of what once was not and soon shall not be. We fall off the edge of the world in being led by God into that union with himself that no ideologically defined goal, no idea, no feeling, no thing finite can reach. And in this passing into God we discover that our prayer is our feasting. In a sacrificial love hidden in faith we are nourished by God's secret presence.

St. John of the Cross devotes the entire first book of *The Ascent of Mount Carmel* to the topic of the purification of bodily desires required to reach a contemplative awareness of our union with God in Christ. He, in effect, then summarizes the first book in Chapter 13, wherein he provides a series of counsels on the purification of bodily desires. He assures us in introducing these counsels that, though brief and few in number, they will, if put into practice, prove to be sufficient in guiding us through the purification of bodily desires on our way to a deeper personal realization of union with God.

His first counsel is one which, in a sense, serves as the basis for all the others. He writes,

> First, have a habitual desire to imitate Christ in all your deeds by bringing your life into conformity with His. You must then study His life in order to know how to imitate Him and behave in all events as He would (*The Ascent,* Bk. I, chap. 13, no. 3).

The path of contemplative prayer is, for the Christian, never anything other than the search for a deeper, more intimate personal realization of our union with God in Christ.

There is, of course, an essential social moral dimension to our imitation of Christ. As Christ's disciples we enter into a community of believers who support us in our efforts to love others as Christ has loved us. But what concerns St. John of the Cross is the interior transformation of the heart that makes Christlike love for others possible. In his second counsel he focuses specifically on the bodily-sensory aspects of this interior transformation.

> Second, in order to be successful in this imitation, renounce and remain empty of any sensory satisfaction that is not purely for the honor and glory of God. Do this out of love for Jesus Christ. In His life He had no other gratification, nor desired any other, than the fulfillment of His Father's will, which He called His meat and food (Jn. 4:34).

> For example, if you are offered the satisfaction of hearing things that have no relation to the service and glory of God, do not desire this pleasure or the hearing of these things.

> When you have an opportunity for the gratification of looking upon objects that will not help you come any closer to God, do not desire this gratification or sight (*The Ascent,* Bk. I, chap. 13, no. 4).

This is a hard saying, one that sounds horribly nihilistic and outright dangerous if put into practice. Coming as it does in the first book of *The Ascent of Mount Carmel,* this "night of the senses" proposed by the saint presents the first major obstacle to understanding his teachings. The positive side of this problematic nature of John of the Cross' writings is that the night of the senses, if patiently examined, can lead the reader to the intuition that then provides insight into the rest of his writings. Indeed, in general terms, it can be said that insight into the spiritual principle underlying the night of the senses provides access to a deeper understanding of all the mystics.

Perhaps the best way to get at what St. John of the Cross means by the dark night of the senses is to begin by listing what he does *not* mean. First, it can be pointed out that we are reflecting upon the words of a saint, a doctor of the church. We can, therefore, have confidence that, if followed to their very bottom, his words will lead us into an insight about the mystery of our life hidden with Christ in God. Therefore, the saint is not writing about anything other than the interior, spiritual dimensions of Christian life.

A second point worth noting is that the biographers of the saint write of his gift for relieving sadness in others. He had a sense of humor which he was quick to use whenever he came upon anyone who was feeling downcast or discouraged. We can only imagine how he would respond to someone who was despondent because of reading his works! Frequently in his writings, the saint affirms the fact that he is writing to lead his reader to a discovery of a great truth which, when freely embraced, sets a person free to be truly happy. In a sense, John of the Cross writes to pose the question: In what does true happiness consist, and how am I to discover it? His answer is that happiness consists in perfect union with God that is discovered in dying with Christ to all the illusions and deceptions that betray this union. He writes to assure us that God in his goodness fills us with an unshakable tranquility and happiness when we remain faithful to this transforming process of sharing in the *kenosis,* the self-emptying of Christ (crucified). Therefore, we can conclude that to read John of the Cross in a manner that leads to feelings of despondency is to misunderstand completely the essentially joyful and liberating nature of his message, which, in the final analysis, is none other than the message of the gospel.

A third observation is that St. John of the Cross is not referring to the appetites themselves. He is not proposing that we somehow isolate ourselves from our senses and bodily desires. As he puts it, "to eradicate the natural appetites, that is, mortify them entirely, is impossible in this life" (*The Ascent,* Bk. I, chap. 11, no. 2). The sensuality of his poetry, the sensitivity with which he refers to the beauty of nature or human intimacy, reveals, if anything, a greatly heightened capacity to respond to all that came to him through the senses. He is, in effect, telling us we do not feel intensely enough. Our vision is dulled, our hearing impaired. He writes to liberate, not suppress the senses.

Nor is the saint advising the beginner to uproot the pleasure that often accompanies the bodily appetites, as if to say, Go ahead, eat a gourmet meal, drink the vintage wine, listen to the soft music—just don't enjoy it! No. Pleasure is inherent in sensory experience. Therefore, to be opposed to pleasure is as meaningless as being opposed to the sensory appetites themselves.

Finally, it can be noted that the saint is not referring

to the daily round of weaknesses and shortcomings that will be with us until our death. John of the Cross writes of the one entering the dark night of the senses that he or she will continue to,

> . . . fall into imperfections, venial sins, and the above-mentioned natural appetites without having advertence or knowledge or control in the matter. It is written of these semivoluntary and inadvertent sins that the just man will fall seven times a day and rise up again (Prv. 24:16). (*The Ascent,* Bk. I, chap. 11, no. 3).

Thus far, the dark night of the senses has been presented as referring to a vital aspect of the gospel message. As such the night of the senses is a source of consolation and not discouragement. It affirms rather than questions the reality and goodness of the senses, accepts rather than opposes sensory pleasure. And it accepts as well our human frailties rather than insisting upon some Olympian conquest over them.

But with this said we are still left with the task of exploring what John of the Cross *does* mean by the night of the senses in which the beginner is instructed to "leave the senses as though in darkness, mortified and empty of pleasure" (*The Ascent,* Bk. I, chap. 13, no. 4). Searching then for spiritual insight into this lesson the saint considers vital to beginners, we can return to the passage quoted earlier in which the beginner is instructed how to be successful in the imitation of Christ, upon which the whole of the spiritual journey is founded:

> . . . in order to be successful in this imitation, renounce and remain empty of any sensory satisfaction that is not purely for the honor and glory of God. Do this out of love for Jesus Christ. In His life

He had no other gratification, nor desired any
other, than the fulfillment of His Father's will,
which He called His meat and food (Jn. 4:34). (*The
Ascent,* Bk. I, chap. 13, no. 3).

Going back through the first book of *The Ascent* of
which the chapter in which this text is found is a sum-
mary, one can discover three themes that provide access
to an understanding of the dark night; namely, reality
and unreality, the union of wills, and equality with God
through love.

Beginning with the theme of reality and unreality, we
can recall the gospel's proclamation of the real in Christ's
words, "The Father and I are one" (Jn 10:30). The
Father and the Son, one in the unity of the Holy Spirit,
constitutes Reality as such. For God is, in Meister
Eckhart's terms, "the all-inclusive order of isness itself."
God is All, the Reality outside of which there is, strictly
speaking, nothing. When Jesus reveals that "He who sees
me sees the Father" (Jn 14:9) he reveals himself as the
manifestation of Reality itself, the one whose identity is
that of being the Father's eternal Word, his perfect self-
expression.

But Jesus did not simply reveal his identity as being
his perfect union with the Father. He also revealed our
identity as being our share in that union. This is why the
disciples at the Last Supper were told to wait for the send-
ing of the Spirit, because, "On that day you will understand that I am in my Father and you in me and I in you"
(Jn 14:20). You will understand that "without me you
can do nothing" (Jn 15:5). This is so because without
Christ we are nothing. The Father creates us moment by
moment through Christ the Word, making us to be
sharers in Christ's glory, which is his union with the

Father. Our reality is then our union with God who is Reality itself. It is our call to share perfectly in the life of Christ the Word.

A passage of the gospels which reveals the mystery of our unreality without God is found in the account of our Lord's temptation in the desert. When tempted by Satan to turn stones into bread, our Lord responded, "Man does not live by bread alone, but by every word that comes from the mouth of God" (Mt 4:4). It is not God's gift of bread that is the temptation, for, indeed, bread is God's word. The Father utters it into being that we might find in it a taste of his sustaining care for us. Nor is the temptation that of the desire to eat, for this too is God's word. It is God who utters into being not simply bread, but what is more our hunger for it as a reflection of our hunger for him. Rather, the temptation is to eat "bread alone," that is, to seek gratification outside of and opposed to God's will.

Only a self alone can eat bread alone. Only a self alienated from its reality in union with God can be seduced into seeking gratification from sensory objects perceived as separate from their Source that sustains them in being, and whose providential care they manifest and incarnate. To eat bread alone is then to feed an illusion with an illusion. It is to gratify an illusory self apart from God with the illusion of gratification apart from God. Of course, at the existential level of daily human experience this way of living is certainly real enough. We really are subject to living in this unrealistic, fragmented search for gratification, as evidenced by the weariness, confusion and blindness in which we so often find ourselves (see *The Ascent,* Bk. I, chaps. 6-10).

In reality there is no bread alone, nor is there a self alone to eat it. There is in reality only God and the Self one with him in the nuptials of his ecstatic love. All of nature shares in this reality. Everything that is is sustained in the unity of God's all-encompassing love.

St. John of the Cross invites us into the dark night of the senses to discover the reality of who we are in union with God calling us to be one with him through Christ the Word. He invites us to accept with a willing heart the death of our illusory clinging to the unreality of seeking self-fulfillment outside of our union with God.

In Chapter 4 of Book One of *The Ascent,* the saint provides a litany of the reality of living in union with God as opposed to the unreality of living in alienation from God's creative, reality-giving will. The litany begins with the theme of beauty:

> All the beauty of creatures *compared* with the infinite beauty of God is supreme ugliness. So a person attached to the beauty of any creature is extremely ugly in God's sight. A soul so unsightly is incapable of transformation into the beauty which is God, because ugliness does not attain to beauty (*The Ascent,* Bk. II, chap. 4, no. 4).

In reality the beauty of creatures cannot be *compared* to the beauty which is God, because their reality *is* their union with God, whose beauty they radiate. The Self awakened by grace to its unity in God sees in the beauty of creatures the beauty of the beloved. As the saint indicates in poetic imagery:

> Pouring out a thousand graces,
> He passed these groves in haste;
> And having looked at them,
> With His image alone
> Clothed them in beauty
> (Spiritual canticle, stanza 4).

In the unreality of separation from God's creative, all-sustaining will, creatures are seen as creatures, not in God, but in themselves, as objects that an illusory self in itself can somehow seize hold of and possess. But "ugliness does not attain to beauty," unreality does not attain to reality. The disunity which is not does not attain to the unity that is. And it is this ugliness, this unreality, this disunity which is negated in the dark night of the senses.

Continuing then in this same vein, by using the imagery found in the rest of this litany of the real, we can reflect on our sitting in contemplative prayer. It is there in our sitting we express most single-mindedly, and therefore most poignantly, our desire to enter into the realization of who we really are in union with God. And it is there in our sitting we express our single-minded willingness to die to all that blinds us to this reality, to all that leaves us the victim of our unreality without God (see *The Ascent,* Bk. I, chap. 4, nos. 4-7):

We sit in the hope of dying to the ugliness of our clinging to the unreality of sensory beauty apart from "the beauty which is God." We sit in the hope of realizing who we are as transformed into that beauty, called to be one with it forever.

We sit clumsily in the coarseness of our alienation from "the infinitely elegant." We sit in the hope of dying to this coarseness, so as to realize God's exquisite art in fashioning us into the perfection of his image.

We sit as victims of the evil of having "set our hearts" on the illusion of a life apart from God. We sit in the graced willingness to die to this evil that the goodness of our life in union with God might be realized.

We sit in the ignorance of our knowing apart from "the wisdom that is God." We sit waiting for God to set us free from this ignorance that "cannot grasp what wisdom is." Sitting in silence, we gently set aside our own knowledge. Like "an unlearned child" walking into the darkness searching for his father who calls to him, we walk on in unknowing. *That is, we leave behind our ideas, our plans, our wisdom by surrendering to the Silence which we intuit to incarnate the wisdom God is.*

We sit in the slavery of seeking a sovereignty for ourselves apart from God. We sit with "a slave's heart," waiting for God to awaken within us "a son's heart," a daughter's heart, set free in the sovereignty of God.

We sit in the torment of our separation from "the delight that is God." We sit in the poverty of our loss of the wealth that is God. We sit as an act of childlike confidence that God's will for us to share in his delight, to be heirs of the wealth he is will be realized within us.

A second theme developed by St. John of the Cross in Book One of *The Ascent* is that of the *union of wills* through which we enter into the reality of our lives in union with God. God does not force the reality of our lives in union with him upon us. He calls us to it. He wills us into being, waiting for us to will the union with himself that he himself wills. For St. John of the Cross it is in the conformity of our will to God's will that our transformation into God takes place. The dark night of the senses is concerned with the senses and bodily appetites as expressions of the will turned either toward or away from divine union. By seeking divine union the saint states that,

> . . . a man's will is so completely transformed in God's will that it excludes anything contrary to God's will, and in all and through all is motivated by the will of God.

Here we have reason for stating that two wills become one. And this one will is God's will which becomes also the soul's (*The Ascent,* Bk. I, chap. 11, no. 3).

To explore this conformity of wills, and how the senses are related to it, we can return once again to the passage in which the saint informs his reader what is required in order to be successful in the imitation of Christ, who is the foundation and the exemplar of our journey toward divine union. The passage reads,

In order to be successful in this imitation (of Christ), renounce and remain empty of any sensory satisfaction that is not purely for the honor and glory of God. Do this out of love for Jesus Christ. In His life He had no other gratification, nor desired any other, than the fulfillment of His Father's will, which he called his meat and food (Jn 4:34). (*The Ascent,* Bk. I, chap. 13, no. 4).

Jesus lived with the Father's presence ever stirring in his heart. He was drawn in everything he did into that intimacy with the Father that is his as Word and ours as persons created to be one with the Father in Christ forever. We do not know the secret urgency with which our Lord was impelled to spend whole nights alone in prayer, where, unseen by every mortal eye, he yielded himself to the Father.

We do not know what it was for our Lord to be swept up in his Father's love, coming to him in a widow offering her last penny, a weeping prostitute, a piece of bread, a glass of wine. We do not know the unseen power that called him up onto the cross, emptied him, leaving him to be as nothing, only to raise him up out of that nothingness into eternal glory.

And yet in this is the goodness and mercy of God revealed to us: The Holy Spirit has been sent into our hearts, awakening us to the Father's call for us to be one with him in Christ. The very love that unites the Father and the Son stirs within us, and with unutterable groanings inflames the will to seek no other gratification than perfect communion with God.

Here is where everything changes, where nothing is the same. Like a fire kindled within, like rivers of living water springing up in the innermost recesses of the heart, we discover that what John of the Cross said of his own life we too can say of ours:

> One dark night
> Fired by love's urgent longing
> —Ah the sheer grace!—
> I went out unseen
> (*The Dark Night,* stanza 1).

It is very personal, something not readily talked about for fear of betraying it with words. But somehow a response is necessary in knowing this: One dark night God came unannounced into my faltering ways. Having fixed his gaze upon me, he reached out and with great gentleness traced upon my heart the sheer grace of an urgency of love for him. This urgency of love is a great consolation, and yet it is as though he traced upon my heart a razor's slash—for it somehow hurts—and will continue to do so until this urgency of love is fulfilled.

Because I am blind, I do not see this touch of love that has claimed my heart. Because my faith is weak I doubt the power that has been awakened within me. Because I am confused by all my compromises and attachments I continue to delay in embracing the wisdom of surrendering completely to this touch. But God never gives up on me, he continues to renew in unexpected ways my awareness of his presence within and around me calling me to union.

This is where the union of wills begins—by becoming silent enough to risk experiencing the full weight of this inner touching of the heart and then to base one's entire life upon it. This is to enter into the inner way that leads to union. Prudence is necessary. One must remain attentive to how God wills us to grow in our daily relationships with others. One must stay rooted in scripture and in the life of the church. One must courageously face one's evasions from the need to grow into a responsible, loving person. But in the midst of all these things, one must step off the edge of the explainable, must risk believing in God, who like an eternal beggar, poorer than poor, waits to find the one who is willing to live for him alone. One must risk entering into the Silence in which one is brought to say, "I am the one for whom God waits. I know it is so, because of the desire for him that he has placed within me."

It is precisely here at this point that St. John of the Cross approaches the beginner with words of encouragement and guidance in following this path of interior transformation that leads to divine union. And in terms of a union of wills, the saint reminds the beginner of a salient characteristic of a lover's heart; namely, its tendency to seek union with the beloved *and nothing else.* A lover's heart knows no rest, finds no gratification, nor desires any other except intimate communion with the beloved. The deeper the love the deeper the realization that everything outside of and opposed to union is strangely, and if clung to, painfully insufficient.

The Hindu saint, Sri Ramakrishna, provides two beautiful images of this aspect of love and how it relates to our love for God. When asked how we are to live in the world, Ramakrishna responded,

> Do all your duties, but keep your mind on God. Live with all—with wife and children, father and mother—and serve them. Treat them as if they were very dear to you, but know in your heart of hearts that they do not belong to you.

> A maidservant in the house of a rich man performs all the household duties, but her thoughts are fixed on her own home in her native village. She brings up her master's children as if they were her own. She even speaks of them as "my Rama" or "my Hari." But in her own mind she knows very well that they do not belong to her at all.

> The tortoise moves about in the water. But can you guess where her thoughts are? There on the bank, where her eggs are lying. Do all your duties in the world, but keep your mind on God.*

Do not forget where your treasure lies. Do not commit idolatry by falling prey to the illusion of allowing any creature, infinitely less than God, to rush into the inner sanctuary of the heart reserved for and created by God alone. Experience life to the full, but do so in fidelity to who you are as one who has been claimed by love. Live in the knowledge that the entire universe is as nothing compared to the beloved—who, in secret, continues to touch the will, inflaming it with desire for union with himself. Trust that God's mercy quickly covers over every isolated act of attachment to creatures. Trust too that your habitual weaknesses, the seven times a day nonsense, is no obstacle to divine union. For God is your Abba, who

*Nikhilananda, trans. *The Gospel of Sri Ramakrishna.* N.Y.: Ramakrishna-Vivekananda Center, 1973, p. 81.

in Christ embraces you in your weakness, calls you to transforming union just as you are.

But every deliberate, habitual attachment to anything less than God must be abandoned, if union with God is to be realized. To find where these attachments lie hidden, ask yourself this: What is there in my life which, if taken from me, would cause me either to lash out in anger or recoil in fear? What am I clinging to in the conviction that it makes me real?

Perhaps the deliberate, habitual attachment is to my health or to my illness. Perhaps it is to my virtue or to my many past sins I am attached. Perhaps I am clinging tightly in a possessive way to a person, a physical object or some spiritual quality, such as the fact that I read St. John of the Cross. Perhaps I am attached to the possibility of my becoming nonattached. In each case the root problem is the same—the tendency to find identity in creatures, to seek one's circumference in the finite. Like a compulsive eater seeking in food the consolation that cannot be found there, we in our sinfulness, "feed and pasture on worldly things" (*The Ascent,* Bk. I, chap. 3, no. 1). We eat the world with our senses, attempting to find in creatures the fulfillment that only union with God can bring.

The dark night in which we are set free from this idolatrous clinging to the finite is a night that begins with fire—the sheer grace of a touch of divine love that enflames the will to seek consummate union with the one who has touched it. In following the promptings of this divine call to union, the heart is left "free and empty of all things, even though it possesses them" (*The Ascent,* Bk. I, chap. 3, no. 4). This is so because all things are now insufficient in being less, infinitely less than the beloved with whom one now wills to be united.

The world is still there. Pleasurable things are still pleasurable. But now a greater unknown, unfelt pleasure keeps stirring in the heart, making every other pleasure to be, by comparison, as nothing. Painful things are still painful. But now the sweet pain of love crucified in emptiness, of love unfulfilled, leaves every other pain powerless to claim one's heart. The beauty of creation is still seen, now more clearly than before, as the beloved's messenger. But now no messenger will do. Only union with the beloved will suffice. The interplay of one's strengths and weaknesses is still very much in evidence. But this too has ceased to become interesting. For, now, by God's grace, the will is conformed to God's will. The union with himself which the Father wills for us in creating us moment by moment through Christ the Word is now the union we ourselves desire.

We cannot understand what this means in conceptual terms. We cannot imagine how much God wills for us to be one with him or how it is that he is transforming our will to resonate with his own. Nor do we have to conceptualize or imagine this divine transformation. Rather, our task is simply to be faithful to it by courageously striving to uproot every deliberate, habitual attachment to anything less than God.

Each time we pray the liturgy of freeing the will from being seduced by the finite begins anew. When we first sit, there is the tendency to be dominated by possessive ego consciousness. We sit entangled in a net of victories and defeats, opinions and apprehensions. At first, prayer itself gets tangled in the net. Each consolation is milked for all it's worth. Each insight noted so as not to become "lost." Each bout with distractions causes discouragement, as does the experience that nothing is happening or that we are praying without getting anything out of it.

And so it goes until grace comes to us in the simplicity of an inner awakening of the heart. Secretly, God's love for us—too deep to feel, too close to see, too tender to endure—inflames the will with the sheer grace of the desire for union. The touch silences us—draws us into that inner Silence in which we spontaneously recognize and follow the voice of the beloved calling us into intimacies unknown. The touch impoverishes us in revealing that what we strive to do with much labor and without success God achieves in us in the twinkling of an eye for his love's sake. The touch transforms us, making our prayer to be a sacrament of our entire life, now given over to divine union. It is not as though one is now perfect, but rather like a homeless pauper who has fallen hopelessly in love, one has become mysteriously enriched by a desire for an ever-deeper intimacy with God.

This transforming desire, being divine, is not seen directly, but its fruits are recognized everywhere. One's relationships with others take on a new capacity for compassion. In and through one's frailties and strengths there is recognized the call to be a benevolent presence, a place in which love finds no obstacle in manifesting itself in the world. There is the freedom to turn a corner to discover someone through whom God calls us to set down the burden of the familiar and the predictable in order to love and be loved in ways not known before.

The fruits of this transformation are seen too in the questions that arise out of nowhere to occasion new, unforeseen encounters with God: If I were to own everything that is, would I have more than I have now? If I were to be stripped of everything, owning nothing, what would I lack? If I were to die now in this moment, would it make any real difference? Would I be any more or less where I really am? Would I receive anything that is not already, eternally, perfectly given to me? Each question engenders anew an empty place into which God lures us so as to unite us more intimately with himself. And so the journey goes, the way becoming always more obscure in an ever more transparent immediacy of Love.

A third theme found in the first book of *The Ascent* is that of the power that love has to bring about "a likeness between the lover and the object loved" (*The Ascent,* Bk. I, chap. 4, no. 3). God initiates this movement toward equality. He is Love, who in creating us as persons calls us to share in the equality of knowledge and love shared by the persons of the Trinity. Our sin is our refusal to accept this divine call to equality with God. Our salvation is that God recapitulates creation in Christ the Word, who became like us so that we might become like him, one with God.

Jesus "did not consider his equality with God a condition to be clung to, but emptied himself taking on the form of a servant" (Phil 2:6). The unutterable groanings of the Spirit within us call us not to consider our inequality with God a condition to be clung to. With the urgency of love unfulfilled God calls us to empty ourselves of our inequality to God (that is to empty ourselves of our attachments to creatures) by becoming servants of the Love that calls us.

The equality with God to which we are called is not a substantial equality. It is not as though God ceases to be God, the transcendent Other, or that we cease to be the creatures of his love, forever dependent on his sustaining, creative will. Rather, the call to equality with God refers to the order of divine love prior to and beyond the order of substantial being. It refers to the order of identity in God in which the Self one with God proclaims "the eye with which I behold God is the eye with which God beholds me" (Eckhart).

The saint concludes the 13th chapter of the first book of *The Ascent* with a mystical poem about this mystery of our union with God in the personal order prior to the substantial order of nature, of all that is this or that. He writes,

> To reach satisfaction in all
> desire its possession in nothing.
> To come to possess all
> desire the possession of nothing.
> To arrive at being all
> desire to be nothing.
> To come to the knowledge of all
> desire the knowledge of nothing
> (*The Ascent,* Bk. I, chap. 13, no. 10).

The created order is the order of things, each limited to being the thing that it is. The divine order is that of God's blessed no-thing-ness. He is the ALL precisely because he is in no way a thing, a being among beings, an object. He contains within himself, as one with himself, the eternal possibility of all things as well as their perfection in him. He is thus the eternal ground of all that is, the Reality of all that is real.

We are God's creatures. Each of us is an individual limited to being the individual that we are as separate from every other individual. We live our lives in a world of things, constantly acting upon and being acted upon by all the contingencies around us. Or so it seems when viewed on the surface.

From the vantage point of faith, however, such is not the case. Religious faith reveals to us that while we are subject to the realm of things we, as God's children, are also called to transcend it. In fact, as enlightened by faith, we hold to an intuitive certitude that our true fulfillment lies not in the realm of things at all, but rather in the realm of the blessed no-thing-ness of God, the All in whose image we are made.

The blessed no-thing-ness of God is given to us and is entered into by love. It is in God's love for us that he calls us to share in his life, and it is in our love for God and others that we enter into the divine life to which we are called. It is in our being transformed by a love not content with things that we come into the blessed no-thing-ness of God.

God gave us one another that we might discover in our love for each other his blessed no-thing-ness. At first, a friendship tends to form because of certain things that each likes about the other. But as the relationship matures each discovers that what unites them as one becomes less and less what can properly be expressed in conceptual terms or objectively accounted for in a list of things that each likes about the other. They discover together the no-thing-ness of love, its power to root the heart in unseen depths that transcend all that is this or that.

To be a disciple of Christ does not mean simply that we follow this anonymous law of love in our love for others. Nor does it mean that we simply add to our love for others a love for all the *things* that God does for us. Instead, it means to follow Christ through our love for others and through our gratitude for all God's gifts into the bosom of the Father, into the inexhaustible ground of no-thing-ness itself. This is done not by any thing that we can do, but by being faithful to the Spirit's promptings within us giving birth to a love that is discontent with things, even the things of God. It means to be content with God alone and to know no satisfaction save union with him in his blessed no-thing-ness.

To sit in contemplative prayer is to turn one's heart toward the blessed no-thing-ness of God. Along the way there are moments of discouragement, but being something each discouragement has not the power to retain us. Along the way there are gifted moments of consolation and insight, but these, being something, have not the power to detour us from divine union. And what of our arrival in him who is all, what of our death or final deliverance? This too is no-thing-ness—a depth of Presence infinitely beyond the realm of gain or loss, of becoming or ceasing to be.

How does this transformation of the heart come about. We do not know, for after all, no thing is happening, no thing is coming about that we can know in conceptual terms. What does it mean to say such things? We cannot say what it means. To attempt to do so is to fall back into the realm of things possessed, the realm of what once was not and soon shall not be. But with a subtle suddenness and always unexpected nearness the blessed nothing-ness of God continues to touch the heart with longing. In a moment of silent prayer, a chance encounter with another, a loss too painful to be fair, the call to union moves us secretly, relentlessly yet further along the way.

There is, it seems, no choice but to trust in God by learning to be patient in the realization that,

> To come to the pleasure you have not
> you must go by a way in which you enjoy not.
> To come to the knowledge you have not
> you must go by a way in which you know not.
> To come to the possession you have not
> you must go by a way in which you possess not
> To come to be what you are not
> you must go by a way in which you are not
> (*The Ascent,* Bk. I, chap. 13, no. 10).

Divine love achieves this in us. It dispossesses us of even ourselves as a kind of thing we enjoy, know, possess and are. What is more it dispossesses us of ourselves as empowered to enjoy, to know, to possess, to be. That is, both possessor and possessed are undone in no-thing-ness. Both the self that would own one's life and the life one seeks to own are undone in the union with God to which we are called.

Every time we waver in the emptiness by clinging to some thing, Love touches us with discontent, telling us that,

> When you turn toward something
> you cease to cast yourself upon the all.
> For to go from all to the all
> you must deny yourself of all in all.
> And when you come to the possession of the all
> you must possess it without wanting anything.
> Because if you desire to have something in all
> your treasure in God is not purely your all
> (*The Ascent* Bk. I, chap. 13, no. 10).

To the ego self incapable of going beyond itself as a kind of thing possessing and being possessed by things, this way of love is naughting and death. It is the stripping away of every thing, until in the end no thing is left. But to our true Self, hidden with Christ in God, the *kenosis* is the way of freedom and fulfillment:

> In this nakedness the spirit finds
> its quietude and rest.
> For in coveting nothing,
> nothing raises it up
> and nothing weighs it down,
> because it is in the center of its humility.
> When it covets something
> in this very desire it is wearied
> (*The Ascent,* Bk. I, chap. 13, no. 10).

To be in the center of one's humility is to be centered in the truth of one's call to intimacy with God. This center is "the stillpoint of the turning world" (Eliot), the hidden axis of the cross around which the wheel of life and death silently turns. As hidden in this axis, this blessed no-thing-ness of God, no thing lifts us up. Every thing perceived as gain is enjoyed in the realization that, being less, infinitely less, than God it is powerless to fulfill us. Thus, all good things are held lightly, possessing them as though we possessed them not. So too, no thing weighs us down. Everything perceived as loss causes fear and pain, but does so in the realization that all loss, including death itself, has no dominion over us. Loss is held lightly in our having been set free from the decay to which all compound things are subject.

Of course, in our frailty, we forget, we fall back over and over into coveting some thing. And each time this happens God's mercy comes to us incarnate in our anxiety, our weariness and discontent. Even as we cling to the gain or loss that has seduced us, God comes to us, speaking to us in our self-betrayal saying: "See. It is true. No thing will do. I and I alone am the beginning, the way, and the fulfillment."

When the spiritual person cannot meditate, he should learn to remain in God's presence with a loving attention and a tranquil intellect, even though he seems to himself to be idle. For little by little and very soon the divine calm and peace with a wondrous, sublime knowledge of God, enveloped in divine love, will be infused into his soul. He should not interfere with forms or discursive meditations and imaginings. Otherwise his soul will be disquieted and drawn out of its peaceful contentment to distaste and repugnance. And if, as we said, scruples about his inactivity arise, he should remember that pacification of soul (making it calm and peaceful, inactive and desireless) is no small accomplishment. This, indeed, is what our Lord asks of us through David: *Vacate et videte quoniam ego sum Deus.* [Ps. 45:11] This would be like saying: Learn to be empty of all things—interiorly and exteriorly—and you will behold that I am God.

St. John of the Cross